"WITH HIS BUNDLE SAFELY ON HIS HEAD HE TOOK
TO THE WATER"

13 DAYS
THE CHRONICLE OF AN ESCAPE
FROM A GERMAN PRISON

BY

CAPTAIN J.A.L. CAUNTER
IST BN. THE GLOUCESTERSHIRE REGIMENT

ILLUSTRATED BY THE AUTHOR

INTRODUCTION

On placing before the public this account of my escape from Germany and some episodes from my life in two prison camps, I feel that I must make clear that it was only due to the fact that I had two definite supplementary objects to attain, that I succeeded in making myself launch out in the following pages.

The first of these objects is to add my quota to the information before the public relating to the treatment and existence of those who, in prisons in Germany, have suffered and are suffering for their country.

My second object is to try to throw a little light on the marvellous spirit of the prisoners as a whole.

Think what it means to be shut up for years under such conditions.

Let me quote the prisoner poet, Lieut. Harvey, who, in *Gloucestershire Friends*, vividly describes what prison means in the following lines:

Laugh, oh laugh loud, all ye who long ago
Adventure found in gallant company!
Safe in stagnation; laugh, laugh bitterly,
While on this filthiest backwater of time's flow,
Drift we and rot till something set us free!

It is always a fight against this sort of thing that the prisoner of war is waging. Some apparently find such a fight difficult, but the majority do somehow keep a hold on themselves and retain their energy and hopefulness.

"Barbed-wire" disease is now officially recognised, and internment in neutral countries of those who have done the longest spells in prison is the outcome of this.

It will readily be conceded that those who keep cheerful throughout their cruel trials display wonderful moral courage. But what about another class of prisoner? The prisoner who tries to escape—is caught—does three months cells—is released—tries to escape again—meets the same fate—and does another stretch of perhaps six months this time—but only goes on trying.

There are some who have spent two and a half years out of three in Germany in cells for attempts to escape. There are many who have made six or seven attempts. I, who only had one determined attempt and succeeded, am able to say it: "These men are of the salt of the earth."

I have heard some chicken-hearted persons who say that nobody ought to try to escape because it might make it worse for those left behind. There is only one answer to that sort of person.

However, it is not a fact that others get punished for the escape of individuals, although it was true on two occasions in 1914; so the question hardly arises.

Very few people in this country seem to realise that the German, being a bully, has the characteristics of a bully. If a strong attitude is taken with him he immediately gives way. Collectively and individually they cannot understand any argument but Force, whether it takes the form of a reprisal or a great attack at the front.

GERMANY

Since my return to England I have often been asked what do the Germans think of the war now and are they hard up for food, etc.

The Germans I talked to were thoroughly fed-up with the war and only wanted peace. This does not mean that they will break out into Revolution. That to my mind cannot come about until the military defeat of Germany is a fact. The Kaiser, not too popular nowadays, would immediately regain his former position in the minds of his subjects could he but secure a peace even partially favourable to the German people. The rulers of Germany know that defeat, or anything like it, would be fatal for them; that is why they will stick at nothing and spare no spilling of blood until they have either won or lost irretrievably. What would a patched-up peace mean? It would mean that Germany would begin building submarines by the hundred for use against us within ten years' time. It would mean just an armistice for a few years and then a renewal of the conflict without Russia and probably many of our other exhausted allies.

The Germans with whom I spoke knew this and looked at the future with open eyes.

I wonder if it is realised how much the British are hated by the Germans? Their hate of us is "Kolossal," to use their own expressive word. Somebody in Germany said that should the Germans ever get into England they would make "Belgium appear like a Garden of Eden in comparison with what England would look like after they had done with her."

It is a German boast that the war has never touched the sacred soil of the Fatherland. The few occasions on which our aeroplanes bombed German towns during my stay there, gave me an excellent opportunity of judging how sensitive they are to this particular form of punishment. The bombing of Karlsruhe and Freiburg caused a scream throughout the west of Germany. I heard the echo of it in the canteen at Crefeld.

When I suggested that London had also been bombed and innocent lives lost, they simply said that that was different. Thus in their minds there are two kinds of law, one for England, the other for Germany. I was very pleased to notice how much less was the effect of air-raids on our civilian population than on the Germans. There is no doubt whatever that the fear of air bombardments is much stronger in Germany than over here.

There is only one way of touching the German mind and that is by the employment of FORCE, Brute Force. It is what he believes in as the medicine for his enemies, simply because he judges others by himself, and knows that he respects that and that only, and therefore applies it whenever possible to others.

It is a pity that our public does not know more of the German mentality. It is a knowledge of this factor that should assist one in having a correct view of things and in understanding German aspirations and methods.

A word about food and supplies generally.

The Germans are extremely hard-up for food. In the Spring of 1917, meat was practically unobtainable. The bread was disgusting and scarce.

Potatoes had to be procured by standing in queues for hours. (This as a matter of fact has been the rule for the last year and a half.)

Mangel-wurzels, swedes, black peas, and turnips form the greater part of the food.

The town of Crefeld in February, 1917, was like a place of the dead, absolutely deserted except at the hour when the workers went home. The shops have practically nothing to sell in their windows. To get a shirt or a towel or any such article, a permit had to be got from the town authorities. Boots were a difficult problem. All the children wore wooden shoes. Leather could not be got for love or money nearly two years ago.

It is extraordinary how the German people put up with their hardships.

People ignorant of the true state of affairs in Germany have sometimes asked me if the Germans are shorter of food and other things than we are. I always have to laugh as the question is so ridiculous to me. There is absolutely no comparison between the two countries.

I often see articles in the papers on the conditions that obtain in Germany, written by persons who know, and I hear people doubt the veracity of them. I can truthfully say that I have not yet seen the article or item of news from Germany which I, from my point of vantage, did not absolutely believe. It is a pity that people will not believe what men who have been in Germany have to say on the subject.

PART I

CHAPTER I
CREFELD

I was taken prisoner at Gheluveld, 31st October, 1914, and arrived at Crefeld prison-camp on the evening of 2nd November with ten other officers brought in from various parts of the Ypres front.

It was the same old story every time that one heard, on asking what had happened in any particular sector of the battlefield.

The impression we got from the sum total of these descriptions led us to think that a German break-through to Ypres and beyond was a certainty during the evening of the 31st.

We had been taken through the German reserves while being transported to the rear, and had seen the thousands of fresh men they had got massed behind their fighting armies. Menin, Wervicq, and other places were packed with troops. Every farm and cottage held its full complement of armed Boches. On the railway, trains passed westwards every few minutes crammed with troops, destined for the Ypres battle.

It was not surprising that we prisoners, who knew the exact strength of the British army, and also the fact that all units were having hard fighting, and that nothing was left in reserve, should feel depressed and wonder if it was possible that the Germans would fail to use their great opportunity.

I have often been asked how our prisoners are treated in Germany. The only correct answer to this is that the treatment varies according to the time and place, and the type of German who comes into contact with them.

In 1914 it was generally the same throughout Germany. In those days the treatment was exceedingly bad. Every prisoner taken then has seen or experienced some brutality or insulting behaviour on the part of Germans.

For my part, I, on first becoming a prisoner, was spat at and called all the choice names their musical language can provide. I saw a British soldier, with a shrapnel wound in the back, made to carry a heavy German pack which bumped up and down on the open wound. This fact was remarked upon by a German private soldier, who, more humane than the rest, protested against this treatment. But the Unter-Offizier would not alter his order and the wounded man had to carry his burden for seven miles or more.

When asked for water at Aix-la-Chappelle railway station, by prisoners who had hardly had a drop to drink for two days, and scarcely a scrap of food to eat, I heard the Red Cross "Ladies"! reply—"For an "Engländer"? Nein!"

At Cologne station I saw the brute beasts of German officials haul three or four of the most miserable British private soldiers they could find, out of the cattle trucks and place them on the platform to be baited by the populace, comprised largely of women. There were German officers on the platform, so there was no excuse; it could have been stopped instantly by them.

There were many other incidents too numerous to mention, but similar and worse stories will be told by the thousand after the war. The treatment of prisoners has steadily improved since those days. No longer do the Germans openly insult and knock prisoners about to the same extent, except in out of the way places and when they have a particularly cowed and defenceless lot to deal with.

I have heard from officers taken prisoners in 1916, that they were reasonably treated when captured. It is much changed now according to general report.

While waiting at Cologne station for our train for Crefeld, we were locked in a cell under the stairs of the station. Although expecting to receive food here and being told that it was with that object that we had been put in this place, nothing of this kind materialised. However, we had the great honour of being visited by a German general and a young female of high rank, who could speak a little English.

This she aired, and asked us several silly questions. She was much taken with S———'s height, comparing him to some Karl or other. It was a kind of private show of the wild beasts at the Zoo in which we acted the parts of the animals.

On arrival at Crefeld station a hostile crowd was ready to receive us, and we were hurried as quickly as possible into the trains waiting there, in order to get us away from the attentions of the populace. As it was, two of the eleven officers in my party were hit with sticks, the wielders of which had pushed their way through the escort of German soldiers accompanying us.

We were not sorry to reach the barracks and get away from these demonstrations of the unpopularity of England in this town. Crefeld, a great centre of the silk industry, had suffered heavily by the entry of England into the war.

Once inside the camp we had time to spare for anything we wished to do, which naturally meant food first, sleep next, and after some time a wash and shave.

The barracks of the Crefeld Hussars, now wired in and used as a prison camp, are large and strongly built. The prisoners occupied three large buildings and a fourth smaller one provided mess rooms and canteen, etc.

There was a gravel parade square in the middle of the ground between the buildings; this we used as a place for exercise. This square was a hundred and forty yards long by about eighty yards wide. It made an excellent association football ground when cleared of big stones, and in the summer, by dint of hard labour, we turned it into a number of tennis courts.

Until he got command of Belgium, Von Bissing—the brute responsible for the death of Nurse Cavell—was the general in charge of the particular army command which included Crefeld in its jurisdiction.

On the walls of the prison camp an order signed by Bissing was posted, which informed all the prisoners that they were the inferiors of all Germans, whatever rank they might hold.

The order also warned us against trying to "evade our fate by escaping." It continued, "The guards are earnest men, knowing their duty." This caused the nickname "earnest men" to be given to them.

I wish Bissing could have known how we laughed at his special order. The Boche has no sense of humour or he could never have put a thing like that on the walls for Englishmen to laugh at and ridicule generally.

For the first year or so, only seven officers were allotted to the smaller rooms and fourteen to the larger ones. But these numbers were eventually increased, first to eight and sixteen respectively, and then to nine and eighteen.

At first we had a cupboard each, but later four had to do duty for seven officers. The beds were iron with wooden planks supporting a hard mattress, sometimes filled with straw or wood shavings, which was changed on one or two occasions.

During the first few months we had only small oil lamps for lighting purposes, at a scale of one per seven officers. It was impossible for everyone to read at the same time. We used to sit over the fire for warmth and the three nearest to the lamp could manage to see sufficiently in the evenings to read the few Tauchnitz editions we had been able to purchase through a tradesman, who was allowed into the barracks twice a week.

As nearly all great-coats and waterproofs had been taken away from prisoners at the time of their capture, we felt the effects of the cold pretty considerably. Roll-calls took place at 8 a.m. and 9.30 p.m., generally out of doors. We often went on these roll-calls in the early days with our blankets over our shoulders. A welcome supply of soldiers' great-coats was sent through the American Embassy about Christmas time. During the first winter there were about 250 Russians, 200 French, 120 English and a few Belgian officers in the camp.

That first winter was by far the worst of the three I spent there. We had not got to understand the true nature of the German official reports, and for some time they depressed us.

Parcels began coming in December, but the Germans made us pay duty on them for a time, and as we had very little money in those days, they were not so welcome as they became at a later date, when the duty was removed.

As time went by, conditions in the camp improved, but until the summer of 1915 we had great difficulty in getting permission to do anything to make ourselves more comfortable. In the early summer of 1915, thirty-five British officers were sent to Cologne to be imprisoned in cells as a reprisal against the alleged maltreatment of German submarine crews. The majority of this number went from Crefeld. After two months or more, the reprisal having ended, they came back, looking very white and ill.

Sometime in the month of June of this year a successful escape was made by three Russians, and three others who got out of the camp the following night were re-caught. Apparently they crossed the Dutch frontier but got tied up in swampy ground and had to return across the frontier into German territory again, in search of a way out of this bad stretch of country. It was while attempting this that they were seen by a German patrol and re-captured.

The whole affair was badly managed. The theory which many prisoners held and worked upon, consisted of allowing each small party twenty-four hours start, so that they might have a good chance of getting across the frontier, some eighteen miles away, before the next lot tried, who if caught at once would cause the Germans to discover the departure of others at the nominal roll-call always held after an attempt to escape. If anyone is missed at these roll-calls the frontier guards are warned by wire.

The frontier is guarded just the same, whether an escaped prisoner is reported "out" or not, so getting away unknown is not a necessity. Of this I am absolutely certain from after knowledge of the conditions, but of course nobody knew definitely what was the best course of action at that time.

The mentality of the Boche, on the subject of escape, is curious. In the early days, anyone who tried to escape and was caught was the subject of particular dislike among the Germans, besides suffering his usual term of punishment in cells.

I suppose becoming accustomed to these attempts altered their point of view, as latterly indifference towards evil-doers of this nature was displayed by them and the punishment term of cells was administered and given with the same lack of interest or emotion as the matron of a boys' preparatory school displays on dosing her charges all round with medicine.

During the first winter in prison we built up a library, which eventually became a large affair with a librarian and a room to itself.

Some prisoners managed to continue playing cards from their first days in prison until I left, and I suppose will continue to do so without ceasing until the day of their release. Personally, after the first year I spent in captivity I hated the sight of a card and played very seldom.

The orchestra, from modest beginnings, grew into a really excellent institution. Most of the instruments were hired from the town of Crefeld.

By dint of asking repeatedly, we persuaded the Germans to allow us to run a theatre, which also developed from an extremely crude state into what was really quite a respectable affair.

The main difficulty with which our theatrical manager had to contend, was the lack of material for "girls" in the caste. However, practise and hard training turned out some passable ones in time. The French were more fortunate in this respect than the English. They are all born actors it seems, and they found two or three really excellent male "actresses." The Russians also produced theatrical displays, but were not so persevering in that respect as the French and British.

Periodically the camp used to be visited by German officers on leave from the front. We used to stare at them and they at us, and beyond the necessary salute, took no particular notice of each other.

One thing about the uniform of German officers drew our attention. Although the top half of them appeared smart enough, they always looked sloppy about the legs. Often one would see a German officer with a reasonably well-cut coat, but his breeches would be perfectly impossible. His leggings were worse than his breeches and looked as if they must have been picked up at a second-hand clothes dealer's. They never fitted, and besides giving their wearers legs the same shape all the way down, generally ended off with their edges half an inch clear of the boots all the way round.

The leather of these leggings looked as if it was made of papier-maché. Being generally of a light yellowish-brown colour they at any rate matched the boots, for the latter were nearly always of that particularly aggressive tone of yellow often seen in the shop-windows in England. The German officer seems to like this colour and has it preserved by his servant, whereas we get rid of it at once.

I suppose these officers in their new uniforms criticised the generally unkempt appearance of the English officers in prison extremely unfavourably, not realising that anything is good enough for a prison, and the less new stuff we got from "home" the less unimportant work we gave to the hard-worked tailors endeavouring to cope with the millions of uniforms required by our growing armies.

In the Spring of 1916 we were allowed by the British Government to give our "paroles" for purposes of "walks" and other recreation.

This enabled us to go to the dentist in the town. This dentist, although extremely short-sighted, did not do such bad work, provided you found the hole for him. He did his best for us and his charges were extraordinarily reasonable. These visits to the dentist were naturally very popular, as they enabled us to see new sights and get away from the horrible prison for a few hours. The dentist scored heavily, as he always had a waiting-list and continuous work to do for the prisoners.

As a man he was about as unfit for war as anyone could imagine, and yet they called him up eventually. Being a weedy specimen, small and pasty-faced, with such short-sight that he had the greatest difficulty in seeing anything, he had been returned as totally exempt time after time by the army doctors. But during the winter of 1916-1917, the weeding-out committee of Germans arrived at Crefeld and once more he was examined. To everyone's surprise, and to his most of all, they passed him fit, and off he had to go. It cheered one up to see them need such a man in their armies.

FANCY PORTRAIT OF "THE CRAB"

The commandant, who, together with the vast majority of Germans, believed in a great German victory over the whole world in 1914, began his career as our chief gaoler as an autocrat of the Prussian type. Various objectionable things were done by his orders. Not the least objectionable of these was the stopping of smoking, when Major Vandeleur escaped in December 1914. After a fortnight we regained our tobacco and were allowed to smoke until a similar episode occurred, when the same penalty was imposed.

Sometime in the Spring of 1915, three French officers attempted to escape, but at the last minute, having already gained the outside of the camp, came back into the prison, and in so doing were fired upon by a German sentry who saw them. As the names of these officers were not known to the German authorities, they ordered a roll-call and demanded their names from the senior French officer. Naturally the request was not granted, so the commandant said that all smoking would be stopped for all officers of the camp, unless the names were forthcoming at once. Again he was disappointed, and the tobacco was once more collected. This time most of the parcels of tobacco were filled with lumps of coal and other unimportant trifles, while we smoked, like schoolboys, on the sly. Up the chimney was the favourite place for this.

During the summer of 1915 the commandant changed his tone a bit, and steadily improved from that time forward. Eventually there arrived a time when we could consider him a fair and just commandant, and although no friend of England or the English, he managed to get on very well with his English prisoners.

The French, however, were never able to satisfy their consciences on the subject sufficiently to look upon him as anything but one of the worst. This was too severe. The commandant complained that when he passed them, they would turn their backs on him, in order to avoid having to salute him.

Relations between the English and the allies were always of the best. About half the English preferred the Russians, while the other half preferred the French.

There were many amusing incidents constantly occurring, if one could raise sufficient sense of humour to enjoy them.

One typical example of the way in which we got some amusement out of our guards happened one morning when a German fatigue party was in the barracks loading up a wagon. One of the men had taken off his uniform cap and hung it up by the entrance to one of the buildings. Along came a certain English officer, interested in anything which might assist him to escape, saw the cap, snatched it up and hid it inside his coat, while passing into the building.

Ten minutes or so later, the work being finished, the German soldier looked round for his cap. Meanwhile, the story of the annexation of the cap had gone the round of the prison, so, when the wretched Boche passed along the front of the building with his bald pate shining in the sunlight, he had to run the gauntlet of a crowd of heads peering from all the windows and roaring with laughter at him.

For a long time, I, like the majority of Englishmen, was in a room half-English, half-French. We really got on very well together, but the usual rock upon which French and English split, cropped up in our case. We English wanted a fair proportion of the windows open; the French on the other hand wanted them shut, complaining of "les courants d'air mortels" (draughts).

A compromise was the only possible solution of this universal trouble. On one occasion our allied friends received a consignment of live snails from France, which they proceeded to cook with garlic on a small spirit stove in our room. The smell was appalling. I had to bolt from the room, although I am not over particular. The odour of snails hung about for days afterwards.

These same friends of ours took up fret-sawing as a hobby. Have you ever tried to live in a room in which five or six fret-saws are working for hours at a time? They used to commence work before breakfast sometimes. However, we stuck it without complaining for months.

We had a most extraordinary prison companion, in the person of a Russian, who received the nick-name of "Cuckoo." This Russian was not really an officer at all, but during the great

Russian retreat from Poland was a transport driver. Finding, or otherwise coming by, an officer's great-coat, he was dressed in it, when taken prisoner with many thousands of others. The Germans, who were not able to prove whether all officers were genuine, naturally concluded that he was one, and took him to an officers' internment camp in Germany. During his wanderings from camp to camp, he one day came to Crefeld. The Cuckoo grew his hair long, abnormally long, so that it fell in a matted mass, reaching to his shoulders. It was said that he had vowed never to cut his hair until the Germans had been kicked out of his village. He was called the Cuckoo, because when one day he had climbed a tree he was asked what he was doing by some officer, and replied that he was a cuckoo. This extraordinary person was not allowed to feed with the Russian officers, as they objected to having him with them. So he had to have his meals between the two services, which were normally within an hour of each other. The English officers belonging to the first service were always late in leaving the table, and so were frequently in the large dining-room when the Cuckoo was fed. It was a sight never to be forgotten. His manner of eating was truly marvellous.

On some occasions dried smoked fish were part of the meals, and the Cuckoo would pounce on these like a vulture and gnaw one, holding it by the head and tail with both hands. This was not his only stunt. Another good one was the way in which he shovelled food down. His hands worked absolutely feverishly to supply his insatiable appetite; great gulps of tea were rapidly interspersed, for lubricating purposes, I suppose. For all that, I can say that I saw him at the bath, which is more than can be said for all the prisoners in the camp.

A really plucky, but at the same time comic attempt to escape was made one Spring by a certain officer, who went by the soubriquet of "Peeping-Tom."

The refuse heaps and dust-bins were cleared out daily by an old German man and a boy, who removed the rubbish in a heavy two-wheeled cart drawn by an old ox. This rubbish-cart in these days used to leave the camp without being carefully searched and was emptied some distance from it. This fact was naturally well known to the prisoners, but the question, which most people took to be unanswerable, was how to remain hidden in the rubbish and yet be alive at the end of the unpleasant journey. It remained for "Peeping-Tom" to think of a gas-mask in connection with this scheme. Borrowing one from an officer, who had been lately brought in from the front, and had retained possession of this article of equipment, he dressed himself in it, and choosing a moment when the German boy was looking the other way, and the old man had departed on some other business, he rushed to the cart and got inside. A well-trained batch of English soldier-servants then arrived, each armed with a bucketful of rubbish which they threw over the top of him, successfully hiding him from view. All would now have been well, had not fate cruelly intervened, in the shape of an old German who worked the bath-house furnace, and who occasionally came out for a breath of fresh air.

Seeing this extraordinary looking object disappear into the cart, the old Boche fetched his cap and went off to the commandant's office to report the strange event. Remarking this, another officer who had been assisting the attempt, walked past the cart and warned "Peeping-Tom" that he had been seen and must get out. Suddenly a horrible looking object rose from the middle of the cart sending a shower of empty tins and other rubbish in all directions. For a moment his peaky masked face peered round, and then leaping from the cart, he went like the wind for the room of a friend in the nearest building. The German boy nearly fell flat on his back from fright when he saw this apparition, and could do nothing to hinder its escape from the cart. The Germans arrived in force shortly afterwards, but their bird had flown. From that day onwards, the rubbish was pierced with spikes every time it passed through the main gate, so that this scheme never had another chance.

During the earlier days of our captivity, impromptu sing-songs sometimes used to take place. On one particular occasion this led to trouble with our prison authorities. Empire-day was a day which could be made something of by the English, as a set-off to the numerous Saints-days and fêtes of the French and Russians.

This particular Empire-day, which we had decided to celebrate as a "jour-de-fête," happened to be the day of the declaration of war between Italy and Austria.

The noise made by the Empire-day celebrators was quite appreciable, and sufficiently loud to reach the ears of the many town-people promenading up and down outside the camp. As these Germans had just heard that their so-called ally and friend, Italy, had declared war on Austria, thus upsetting German calculations, they were very angry and depressed. On hearing these sounds of cheerful voices and other manifestations of joy they naturally concluded that our Empire-day celebrations had been especially arranged in order to celebrate the entry of Italy into the war, which fact, combined with their feeling of depression and indignation at what they termed Italian treachery, made them wild with rage, and complaints were sent in to the commandant, who believed also that the noise had been due to a celebration in honour of Italy. It was only after most persistent declarations on the part of the British senior officers, that it was at last satisfactorily explained to the commandant.

On the whole we were exceedingly fortunate in our German officers at Crefeld. One of them, however, was a most ludicrous person. He was nick-named the Crab, on account of his gait. He wore cuffs, which always asserted their independence from his shirt, when he raised his hand to the salute.

This Crab was a fool in his dealings with the prisoners, and various little incidents occurred between him and his charges. On one occasion the order against smoking on parade was re-read to the prisoners, and then the German officers kept their eyes open for smoke for a time after this.

The Crab one day saw an English officer smoking and took his name, with the result that the victim got three days cells. In the course of his campaign against smoking, he next came up against the French.

One of these was observed to be smoking and accused of it. However, he declared his absolute innocence and the Crab was non-plussed. On looking round he found that the whole crowd of Frenchmen were smoking, and roaring with laughter at him. This was too much for him to tackle and he gave it up.

Occasionally our allies received him with a chorus of coughs or suppressed cheers if he came on parade late.

A very fine attempt to escape was made by a naval officer, who used the Crab as his model. One evening, knowing that the Crab was busy in the camp and would not be passing out of the Commandantur gate for a few minutes, the Naval officer, dressed *à la Crab* to the last button, presented himself at the first barrier and got easily through without causing any suspicion. At the next gate, however, the sentry, as a matter of form, asked him for his pass, but unfortunately, not being conversant with the language, he was unable to understand what was required of him, otherwise a word in answer and the production of anything at all resembling the pass might easily have sufficed to allay the man's suspicions. Instead of which the sentry had to repeat his question several times, each time becoming more suspicious of this strangely silent German officer.

It wasn't very long before they discovered the trick which was being played on them and arrest quickly followed. The commandant, it was said, was extremely amused over the whole affair, and made the naval officer show him how he had copied the Crab walk.

He then sent for the Crab, who came to his office to find his double staring at him. The commandant roared with laughter, but the Crab only vouchsafed "very clever" in English as his remarks on the subject, looking very fed-up the while.

All the German employees in the prison used to laugh at the Crab, so this little masquerade caused a good deal of amusement among them.

We were always hearing rumours from someone who claimed to be in the know, about the mobilisation of the Dutch army and a rapid attack on Germany.

This interested us very much of course, as we had visions of being released by Dutch cavalry. However—cheering as these rumours were at first—they became decidedly unpopular when nothing ever happened according to the programme of the rumour.

Sometimes we heard of misgivings in the town when our offensives were stretching the German armies to cracking point. The people didn't believe their official reports without applying a grain of salt to them first, on many occasions. The *Times* was largely read in the town, and I have heard it actually said by a German that he read it so as to get news of the war,—the German papers containing nothing but stuff entirely favourable to the Fatherland.

There was an official report issued by the Great Headquarters every afternoon and this appeared in the *Extra Blatt*, a yellow sheet of paper specially printed. This *Extra Blatt* used to be carried past the prison by an old Boche, who always shouted the same thing—"heavy losses of the English, French and Russians." At last, after hearing him daily for two years or more, the prisoners began to assert themselves, and he was received with cheers, which daily grew louder, until the commandant ordered that the old man should not come past any more and give opportunities for the prisoners to practise their sarcasm at the expense of the communiqués of the Great Headquarters.

The reports about the Jutland battle sent the Germans into a great state of excitement. At first they were very happy, while we said very little to those Boches we met about the camp. A day or two later their joy was rather more assumed than real, until nearly a week afterwards, the sudden marvellous discovery by the German authorities that they had lost some more ships, and the consequent admission of this unfortunate little fact, finally wiped out altogether the dreams of a German domination of the seas, which many deluded people seemed to consider a "fait accompli" after that battle. It was then our turn to smile and drop insinuations and hints that probably their authorities could tell them more if they liked.

Of course we were told what would happen to England when the submarine campaign began. The Unter-Offizier in charge of the parcel room informed us with great glee that the English would be unable to receive any more parcels. Although pooh-poohing his suggestions many prisoners had secret fears on the subject.

There was great excitement in Boche circles when the first batch of parcels bearing postmarks of a later date to that of the first day of the unlimited submarine campaign arrived in the camp. This did not look a all like a complete blockade of England!

After careful thought a satisfactory explanation was forthcoming from the "under officer." "Of course the English postal authorities must have faked the postmarks in order to cause these very misgivings to arise in the minds of true Germans"! Again he and his satellites were able to look on the bright side of things. But not for long did their joy last. The steady stream of incoming parcels continued and joy gave way to sulkiness and then disillusionment in the minds of those Germans who saw with their own eyes. Depend upon it these men told others what they had seen and so it spread. All the same they still imagined, in May, 1917, that we had far less food in England than was really the case.

Talking about food reminds me of the behaviour of the Crefeld children when we prisoners went out for walks on parole. Although undoubtedly brought up upon ideas of hate against England, and presumably thoroughly informed of the odious natures of all Englishmen, these children very soon forgot their lessons and rapidly became great friends with the prisoners— English, Russians, French, Belgians and Arabs alike. Of course to a certain extent their behaviour was due to their hopes of getting odd bits of chocolate or a biscuit or two from their enemy friends. It was not unusual to see the "Walk," generally consisting of about forty prisoners, returning with a crowd of kids of all kinds and description hanging on to its edges. Their usual practice was to get hold of a prisoner's hand and trot beside him, asking sometimes for chocolate and occasionally for old tennis balls.

These children's disregard of the attitude, which the war lord has decided must be displayed against the English, was not allowed to continue unchecked. I expect the children were the subject of a special army order, as they suddenly ceased to join us in our walks, and the usual crowd of urchins who stood for hours in the road outside the barracks in the hopes of having something thrown out to them, were chased from their points of vantage and silence once more reigned in the one time noisy road.

On special occasions the schools were given holidays by orders from headquarters. A victory or the occupation of a town was always commemorated in this way. On these occasions, the headmaster or mistress would march the school past our prison and order the kids to sing patriotic songs. We always laughed at them, and the girls would sometimes forget to sing and would wave their handkerchiefs to us instead, causing their bear-leaders to get wild with rage. Eventually when the Germans got tired of victories and wanted food instead, their holidays ceased and we no longer had to listen to shrill voices shrieking "Die Wacht am Rhein" or "Deutschland über Alles," time after time *ad nauseam*.

It was extraordinary how the feelings of the German people changed towards us while at Crefeld. At first nothing was too bad to say or do to the captives of the Kultur nation, but it is marvellous what a good blood-letting and perpetual food shortage has done for them. So tame did they get that our windows, at first only open at the very top and all covered with white paint, were eventually made so that one could sit and look out quite easily. No fist shaking or gestures of hate were made by the time the windows were allowed open, so prisoners and Boche civilians simply stared at each other quite peaceably.

There was one thing that specially worried us in the camp. By some means or other all attempts to escape by digging tunnels were discovered. Although the foundations of the prison buildings were literally honey-combed with tunnels and attempts were made without number, never once did one succeed.

Most ingenious efforts were made, but despite the most rigid secrecy and the utmost caution, sooner or later in would come a search party and go straight to the scene of the excavation and often catch the diggers red-handed. It was believed that there were spies among the prisoners; at any rate everything that went on was known in the commandant's office sooner or later. The members of one party on being caught were actually complimented on their fine work by the Boches, who were full of joy naturally at having found the tunnel.

For many months before we left Crefeld the Germans used to search the ground floor rooms and cellars daily. Not infrequently they would pay two or three visits to the cellars in one night. Their searching included tapping the walls, ceilings and floors for hollow places. Periodically a search for the earth excavated from these holes and hidden away, would lead to the Boches discovering many hundredweights of sand and rubble stowed away safely.

Searches were sometimes made in our rooms for articles of contraband. Civilian clothes, and maps, compasses and various tools were the chief objects of interest to them. These searches on some occasions were extended to the persons of the prisoners, especially after an order forbidding the possession of real German money had been issued. Of course none of us liked being searched and we showed our searchers pretty clearly what we thought of the whole affair. I must say that the commandant did not order many searches and probably those that did occur were due to the orders of a superior.

These searches were usually carried out by the under-officers and men of a different unit from that which guarded the camp, in order to prevent those who were quite friendly to us among the prison guards letting us off too lightly.

During 1915 we were all inoculated and vaccinated against a number of diseases. In all we were each punctured seven times. Many prisoners objected to these measures and did their utmost to avoid being done. The German authorities caught the majority and treated them to these unpleasant attentions however.

The inoculation was a comic sight. One after the other the prisoners filed past the doctors, who worked automatically at their pricking job. It often was a case of almost leather punching when the tough skins of some of the rougher types of prisoners had to be pierced. The needles were far from sharp, and I believe had to be constantly changed.

Small parties of prisoners were constantly leaving and arriving at the camp. This was done, so it was generally thought, to let the people see prisoners being taken about and make them imagine that the German armies were always taking new batches.

New arrivals from the front were sometimes brought in, and we would generally worry the lives out of them for their first few days, asking for news of all kinds. Hardly ever were they able to tell us anything we did not know from the newspapers, but it often happened that all sorts of wild rumours arose from the remarks of fellows who were simply badgered into saying things they did not really mean or had not thought over thoroughly.

Early in the Spring of 1917 the Germans brought a hundred odd mercantile marine officers and men from Karlsruhe to our camp at Crefeld, with what object nobody rightly knew. These men had been through a very bad time and were very pleased to get to a camp where there were English army officers. The majority of them had been captured by the *Moewe*, and some of them had been in her for weeks while she cruised about sinking other ships. They had been half-starved and had very little clothing with them. In several cases the Germans had sunk their ships so quickly that the wretched crews had had no time to put on any of their clothing and had had to take to the boats in whatever garments they were wearing at the moment.

When they arrived at Crefeld they were received by the military officers and had a breakfast given them at once. They were extraordinarily pleased to get some decent food, and we so arranged it that they never lacked English food with which to augment their camp rations while at Crefeld.

In connection with this, the Germans were very amusing. They expressed their astonishment that officers of our army should take so much interest in British mercantile marine common seamen as to provide them with food and actually wait on them at the first decent meal they had seen for months.

A collection of clothes of all descriptions was made, and most extraordinary sights were to be seen as the result of this. Stokers promenading in the uniforms of Guards officers, and ship's boys in huge "British Warms."

I think the Germans had hoped to annoy us army officers by this introduction of merchant seamen. If this was so they failed utterly to achieve their object. The greatest good feeling existed between the two lots in the camp, and after three or four weeks the merchant sailors were removed to another camp where I am afraid they were less comfortable. The Germans were not the only surprised people over this affair. The French, although Liberty, Equality, and Fraternity is their national motto, were very astonished at the way in which good fellowship and camaraderie was fostered between army officers and merchant seamen.

When the Russian revolution broke out, we all wondered how the Russians in the prison camp would take it. The majority of them seemed to have very little decided opinion on the subject, but were generally inclined to think it a good thing for their country. It was then that we were told that the Russians were all to be sent to another camp, which made the whole camp think furiously as to the reason for this move of the German authorities. Was it peace in sight and the prisoners were to be concentrated in camps by nationalities near the frontiers of neutrals bordering their own countries preparatory to the general exodus at the end of the war? Did it mean a separate peace with Russia?

These and other theories were discussed backwards and forwards. Eventually the Russians went and many of us were very sorry to lose them, as it meant a loss of all means of continuing to learn the language from their Russian friends. Two hundred English arrived from Gütersloh in their place, and then the departure of the French began.

The leave-taking between the French and English was very cordial and annoyed the Germans very much, as while the former went from us we all sang the "Marseillaise." The English continued to sing it until the French were out of sight along the road to the station. Then we became an all English prison-camp. There seemed to be no room to move, as everyone was out of doors, and a great percentage of the Russians and many of the French had kept to their rooms a great deal.

We were only about six weeks in this state, as in May once again the Germans turned the camp upside down, this time ordering its complete evacuation by all the English.

CHAPTER II

THE MOVE TO SCHWARMSTEDT

Many and varied were the aims ascribed to the Boches when the news of the move from Crefeld, ordered in May, 1917, reached the ears of the prisoners.

We were divided into parties of varying sizes. My party was the strongest, consisting of four hundred officers and about seventy soldier-servants.

The greatest secrecy was displayed as to our destination by the Germans, and all sorts of places were mooted as possible by the prisoners themselves.

Shortly before we had heard the news of our impending departure, a strange thing happened. A battalion of young German soldiers marched into the German half of the camp, and very soon after their arrival we were astonished to see another line of sentries posted round the camp outside the barbed-wire fence.

These sentries were only twenty yards apart and were dressed in active service uniforms. In addition to these, machine guns were posted at each corner of the camp so as to command the roads running past it. These precautions were taken a day or so before May 1st, the day when the Social Democrats were to have labour demonstrations throughout Germany.

We were naturally extremely interested and wondered what was to happen.

These German soldiers were far from being on the best of terms with our old Landsturm men, who continued to carry out the usual guard duties as they had done previously.

Nothing else happened beyond the arrest of five civilian Germans who were hanging about the entrance to the prison. Why they were suddenly seized and flung into cells no one rightly knew, but we concluded that it had to do with these same May 1st demonstrations.

The preparations for the great exodus from the camp were full of comic and sometimes almost tragic incidents.

Some prisoners, who had taken the trouble to try to make their rooms comfortable when the camp became all English, were particularly savage over the move, and took care that nothing which they were unable to take away should be left to be sold again to another batch of prisoners at a later date. There was a considerable quantity of live stock of various kinds in the camp, and measures for the transportation of these furred and feathered belongings had to be undertaken. The rabbits had to have special boxes made for them so that they could be carried by hand.

These rabbits had been in existence some six months at Crefeld and were very prolific breeders. They provided many an excellent meal for their owners and were objects of great interest, being watched by a small crowd of the prison inhabitants every day.

Quite a number of canaries, a dog or two and a cat, were also in the camp, and would have to be taken away by their owners.

We were told that our heavy baggage might in due course follow us to the new prison camps and that we could take one box each, which was to accompany us. Of course we all had accumulated much more stuff than would go into one box, and much grousing and desperate thinking was the result of this order.

The commandant promised to have our special boxes of tinned food sent on to us as soon as possible after our departure. Although many of us never expected to see the things again, he kept his promise, greatly to the delight of everyone. These food boxes arrived some three weeks after we had got to the new camp.

On the last evening at Crefeld, definite "move" orders were issued and our names were called by parties. I was detailed for No. 2 camp, which was to have over half the 750 officers at that time at Crefeld. Another party consisted approximately of three hundred officers, and the remaining fifty or so were distributed among two or three other new camps.

Owing to finding out that five or six officers were missing at the final roll-call, another nominal roll-call was ordered that evening in order to ascertain the names of those who were missing. The Crab was in charge of this roll-call, and he stood at the opening of a wire netting fence dividing two tennis courts, while the English officers answered their names and filed past him. Muddles very soon occurred, and what with officers who had already answered their names wandering back among the uncounted ones, so as to answer to the names of those missing, and the mistakes which naturally occur in calling over the names of 750 officers of another nationality, the Germans were bamboozled, and had no idea what they were doing. This roll-call was a fearfully slow one, and it became dark before two thirds of the officers had passed through the opening.

Now, of course, no certainty of keeping those counted from those uncounted could possibly be assured, unless a large number of soldiers were employed to prevent persons slipping from the counted crowd to the uncounted crowd. Accordingly a strong force of German soldiers was sent for, and for some reason or other they made matters worse instead of better.

This state of affairs continued for some time, until someone applied a match to an old broom found on a tennis court. It made an excellent torch and others quickly emulated his example. This was followed by a wild throwing about of these flaming missiles, and it not infrequently happened that one of them pitched extremely near a German soldier forming one of the cordon round us. This sport gave place to bonfires. In a moment some old benches were torn up and three or four fires started. This roused the Boches and they cleared the bonfire stokers away and proceeded to trample out the flames, amid the laughter of all the prisoners. The alarm was sounded on a bugle, and yet another small army of soldiers arrived on the scene, but they did not tackle the largest bonfire which burnt merrily on undisturbed.

It was a weird sight. The red flames lit up a wide area, in which the greater part of the prisoners were strolling about surrounded on all sides by German soldiers in field gray uniforms and carrying rifles. However, the whole affair was only due to over-boisterous spirits, and there was no bad feeling displayed towards the Germans, who very wisely did not interfere to any great extent. When the order to disperse to our rooms was given the prisoners went off quietly enough and the whole affair died out without any trouble occurring. However, at times it had been touch and go, whether the Boches would fire at us.

The hour for parade next morning was extremely early, and we had to wait for hours before we eventually moved off. Prior to leaving the camp our personal baggage, which we were to carry by hand, had to be searched. A large number of young German officers and *Feldwebels* were brought into the camp to carry out this task. They were quite civil and polite and got through their job fairly quickly.

My party was the first to move out of the camp. We then found we had to walk to the station, a mile or so away. It was now that many discovered what a quantity of baggage they had got with them. Everyone had been under the impression that we should go by trams to the station, and consequently had much more to carry than they would have had if a walk to the station had been expected.

It was an awful procession. Every fifty to a hundred yards the column had to halt while bags were changed to the other hand or bundles re-adjusted. We walked four abreast and on both sides of each four was a German soldier.

It was an absolute nightmare. Some prisoners threw some of their belongings away, and a few sat down unable to move a yard further without a rest. At last, after an absolutely agonising time, we reached the station. We were put in the carriages four at a time, with three to four German soldiers in each carriage with us. In my carriage there were four Germans, one of them an Unter-Offizier. The Germans appropriated the corner seats, to prevent us being near the doors. This of course allowed the four of us to play bridge in the middle of the carriage.

Eventually the train moved out of the station and we saw our last of Crefeld. Extraordinary as it may seem, we were positively annoyed at leaving; far from being keen on seeing new places and settling down in new environments, the majority would have preferred to remain in the same old groove for the whole term of their imprisonment. Time seems to go by much more quickly when nothing happens to mark its flight. The two and a half years spent in that prison had slipped by without milestones and it was extremely hard to realise what the two and a half years really meant. One sometimes felt that life previous to the war was really the invention of a dream. It often seemed to one that "prison" was the natural state of existence and anything outside of it unnatural. Perhaps the animals at the Zoo have the same impression of the outside world.

On settling down for our journey to that unknown destination, we had an opportunity of studying our guards. They were men of about thirty years of age and had all been to the front for long spells. For several hours they were very sulky and only answered our remarks and questions in monosyllables.

When we reached Essen they expanded a little in order to point out to us what a wonderful place it was. It certainly was wonderful. Miles of workshops and factories, and in many of them one could see guns, new, old, and damaged, lying about. The Germans in our carriage were evidently proud of this place and talked quite a lot about it, using many adjectives of the "kolossal," "wunderschön" type. We, of course, told them that we had hundreds of places in England of a similar nature and that they would one day see their wonderful Essen burnt to the ground. We thought naturally of air raids on Essen, and in view of the bombing of this place early in the war, we carefully examined it, and came to the conclusion that a bomb would be bound to hit something of importance there, so close together are the various workshops jammed.

At Gütersloh station we slowly passed a train conveying a German battalion towards the West front. We were able to examine the men well. This particular battalion consisted of very fine looking men, but there was no "Joy in the War" expression, as the German papers call it, on their faces, and they were not singing or shouting the incessant repertoire of the front-going German soldier. In fact they looked resigned to their fate, and took very little notice of us. Of course we talked to each other about "Kanonen Futter" for the benefit of the guards in our carriage.

On clearing out of Gütersloh we decided to have a meal. As we had prepared for two or three days in the train if necessary, we had plenty of food with us. It was with great curiosity that we covertly watched our German guards when we produced white bread and tinned beef sent from England. It was evidently a great surprise for them, and they could not help showing their astonishment in their faces. It did not look to them as if England was starving if white bread could still be made, and as for the meat, they had not seen so much during a whole week as we each proposed to eat at one meal.

They had had a meal themselves just before we began ours, so we had been able to estimate what had been given them as their rations. It was very scanty and the small quantity of bread was exceedingly poor looking. In the hopes of getting them to talk a bit, we offered them some beef and a little bread. They accepted with alacrity and became friendly from that moment, telling us all sorts of things that interested us exceedingly.

Apparently, they in common with the majority of Germans, had mistrusted and even feared their English prisoners up till then. Very probably they had all been warned to be suspicious of us, and given to understand that we might overpower them at any moment and escape from the train. There must have been some such fear in the minds of the senior German officers, as there were machine guns on the train in addition to four hundred armed soldiers.

The under-officer told me that he had been wounded twice and been on the Russian front for a very long spell. He had also been on the West front in 1914, and I discovered that he had been in an attack on the very trenches occupied by my brigade near the Chemin des Dames on the Aisne. He had no hesitation in saying which was the nastiest front. He was absolutely fed up with the war, as were the others in the carriage. They asked us when we thought the war would end, and out of principle we said in a year to two years' time. I was often asked the same question while at Crefeld and always answered—"a year or more." This seemed to depress them and they used to blame England for being the cause of the war going on so long. Nearly every day I went to the canteen, and, according to my usual custom, talked to the German soldiers doing duty as salesmen there.

The war was always the subject of conversation and I generally asked them, laughingly, when the great promised defeat of England was going to come off. One day, one of them became quite serious and leant across the counter to me and said in a low tone so that only I could hear—"Germany will never defeat England." As an afterthought he added, "but England can never defeat Germany." I laughed and told him to wait.

It was extremely interesting to observe the gradual taming of the Boche.

In 1914 he was intoxicated with victories actual and prospective; 1915, confident but a little more calm; the big talk of capturing London, etc., had died down by then; 1916, general depression, and towards the end of the year actual and open fear for the future and hate of the war was to be observed among the soldiers and civilians of the lower orders.

By the Spring of 1917, real anxiety about the coming summer's fighting began to be evident, which was partially relieved by the events in Russia and the great promises and hopes held out to them by the submarine warfare.

Their behaviour towards us followed the same gradual scale. At first, bullying, truculent and brutal, they became more docile as time went on, until when we left Crefeld in May 1917, their behaviour was not so far removed from what one had a right to expect from prison guards and officials towards their officer prisoners.

Although the guards in our railway carriage had become quite friendly by now, they did not relax their vigilance, and it was quite evident that they would not sleep all at the same time during the night which was approaching.

I watched very carefully that night, but never once did I catch them all unconscious at the same moment.

There can be no doubt whatever that they had had very stringent orders on the subject, owing probably to the escape of nine British officers from trains in the last three months.

The same watchfulness was displayed by the Germans throughout the train, as we found out on comparing notes afterwards.

The journey continued throughout the next day and we passed through Minden in the late afternoon.

We had now made up our minds that Stralsund, one of the rumoured destinations, was to be our new "home." Great was our surprise when we found that our train had stopped at a small town called Schwarmstedt, in Hanover, and that our new camp was some eight miles from there. The guards got out and formed a close cordon completely round the train and we were told that we were not to be marched off till daybreak. The German soldiers from our carriage not employed on this cordon duty fetched us water at our request and we settled down to sleep for a few hours until the time for moving came. We were turned out of the train at 3 a.m. and after being formed up in fours we waited for an hour or so.

We had a grand opportunity of studying the Prussian method of enforcing obedience and smartness in the men during this wait. A captain and a sergeant-major kind of man, fairly screamed at the privates. On several occasions, livid with rage, one or other of them rushed at some hapless wretch and roared at him in sentences containing very choice German words—hardly of the endearment variety.

Our carriage guards had previously told us that the major, captain and sergeant-major were "Schweine" of the worst type, but that the lieutenant was liked well enough. We could now judge for ourselves.

At last we got the order to move off, our hand baggage being left behind to be brought up by a miniature railway train especially constructed for the purpose of supplying the prison camps.

The camp with several others, as we found out afterwards, was situated on the Lüneburg Heide, some eight miles east-north-east of the town of Schwarmstedt and five or six miles on the Berlin side of the river Aller.

Crossing the river and leaving the valley through which it flowed, we quickly entered a wild tract of country, through which the only road was a rough cart track. The soil was peaty with a deep layer of sand and black dust on the top of it. For the first two or three miles we passed through several very fine pine forests interspersed with young plantations and rough scrub.

This type of country gave way to a flat marshy-looking area covered with rank vegetation and stunted fir-trees. Streams and ditches cut up the land, and it struck one as being a very wet place even in the summer, in winter it would probably be a swamp.

At last we reached the camp and found ourselves looking at a collection of wooden huts with tarred felt roofs, surrounded by a barbed wire fence, seemingly planted at random in the midst of the wildness.

CHAPTER III

SCHWARMSTEDT CAMP

Our first sight of this camp hardly encouraged us to think that we were going to a better place than Crefeld. An ominous silence fell upon the incoming prisoners! And it was a particularly sulky lot who faced the new commandant when he had them formed up in front of him.

He admitted the bad state of the camp in his very first speech, and hoped that we would put up with it as he himself was powerless to alter matters.

On being dismissed, we went off to our rooms and very soon found out all about our new prison.

Imagine dirty sand, covering a layer of peat with water two feet underneath it, enclosed with a barbed wire fence. In this area put four long low wooden huts with tarred felt roofs, three much smaller ones, three pumps, a long latrine, a hospital hut and some cells, and you have the sum total of the buildings in the camp.

The three long low huts held 390 officers, each hut divided roughly into eight to ten rooms. Many of the rooms held sixteen officers, and so crowded were the beds in them that three pairs had to touch in many instances, despite repeated and varied ways of re-arrangement being tried.

The latrines were very close and handy, so much so in fact, that their ends came to within ten paces of the living-rooms at the end of two of the huts. As the latrines were never cleared out, the atmosphere in these near huts was something too appalling for words, especially if a west wind was blowing.

The drinking-water had been passed as fit for human beings by the German sanitary authorities. For all that, the majority of us only drank tea and coffee, etc., requiring boiling water. The water was brownish and smelt abominably.

We became expert laundry hands, as we had to wash our own clothes, and so learnt the art from experience.

Many of the prisoners were able to see the comic side of life in this place fortunately, and so made the best of a bad job.

As the bath-house was outside of the wire fence, we could only get to it by going on parole, or by being marched out in groups. This naturally meant that the turn for baths did not come round too often. If one refused to give parole for this purpose, a bath could be got twice a week with luck.

The natural outcome of this was that everyone used to bath under the pumps which were situated between the living-huts. It was a common sight to see between twenty and thirty naked figures throwing water over each other round the pumps.

It was absolutely impossible to play tennis or football in this camp, as there was no space in which to do such things. The little ground lying between the living huts had been planted with vegetables by the Germans before our arrival. It was against all orders to walk across this ground. A Belgian private soldier, acting as officer's servant in the camp, did so once, and was banged into cells for his offence. No officer was put in cells for this, but that was not due to the lack of opportunity. I think the Germans did not want to cause trouble with their English officer prisoners, so refrained from rash acts of this nature.

As we had been allowed to take only one box with us from Crefeld, some officers had purchased huge baskets in the canteen into which they had crammed great quantities of luggage.

When these baskets were unpacked, the German authorities decided that they were too big to remain in the rooms and so ordered that they should be removed from the camp to a store shed outside the wire fence.

Three officers availed themselves of this fact and hid themselves inside the baskets, arranging that strong English soldiers should carry them out, pretending that they were empty and put them with the other large boxes in the shed. Thus the officers would get outside the camp and eventually get away from the shed by night.

All went well at first. The baskets were outside the gate, and merrily moving off towards the shed, when the Boche officer called upon the soldiers to halt, and decided that as the soldiers were needed for other work the baskets were not to be put in the store room till after five o'clock. Down went the baskets on to the ground and were then massed near the German sentry on gate duty. As it was only two o'clock and fearfully hot, the wretched inhabitants of the baskets had a very poor time of it waiting till five.

One of the three did not keep still and we could see the wicker-work straining from his movements. Awful squeakings and scratchings came from this basket, and although we tried to drown the noise by talking and shouting near the gate, the German sentry must have heard something and became suspicious, as he stood by them and looked carefully at each in turn.

At last they were taken to the store. What really caused their recapture I don't know, but it appeared to be due to one of them showing himself at the window of the store-room some three hours later. They had to be careful to arrange it so that one of the baskets could be cut open from the inside, and the others could then be opened with the keys that the occupant of this basket had on him.

At about eight o'clock the German officer arrived, followed by a guard, went straight to the store-room and captured all three, who by this time had been out of their baskets for hours. We next saw them marched off to cells, where they were to do five months in solitary confinement.

We had not been thirty-six hours in this camp before three officers did get away. Crashing along a ditch, they cut the wire and got through the hole which was in the fence opposite the nearest clump of undergrowth to the camp.

How the Germans did not hear them crashing into these bushes I cannot conceive, as I myself heard them seventy or eighty yards away. These three were away about ten days before being caught. Not very long after their exit the German sentry noticed the hole in the wire and so that chance was spoilt for anyone else. The clump of bushes, which had been so useful to the three escapers, was cut down by order of the commandant, and after that a hundred yards of open clearing surrounded the wire fence, making a good field of fire for the sentries.

Owing to the sandy nature of the soil, which had all the dirt-causing propensities of coal dust and none of the advantages of clean sand, we had to be constantly washing our feet if they were to be kept clean at all. Many prisoners, realising what a lot of laundry work wearing socks in this dusty place meant, discarded their use altogether and simply wore football shorts and shoes, with an old shirt as top-wear.

Our rooms were perpetually in a filthy state. As soon as they were brushed, in came more of this sandy dust. A wind made life unbearable.

These conditions are those of summer, winter will mean a different tale. The open ditches, dry on account of the drought when I left, are hardly there as ornaments, but in all probability are filled to over-flowing with the surface water from the camp, when the rainy months come along.

At the end of the camp was a space wired off from the rest of the ground for the use of the soldier servants. There was a wooden hut similar to those occupied by the officers, which did duty for the housing of the men. In this wooden hut about 200 soldiers, of all kinds and descriptions, were packed—Russians, French, Belgians, and English, and not a few half-German half-Russian Jews.

These latter men were allowed great freedom by the Germans. There was no fear of them escaping, so they walked in and out of the camp whenever they wished to do so, as far as we could see. They were hardly trusted by the rest of the prisoners, who had good reason to know what useful sources of information these persons are to the German camp authorities.

I went to these quarters of our soldiers several times, although officers were not supposed to do so. But if no coat was worn, it was impossible for a German sentry to tell who was an officer or a private, so we used to adopt that plan if we wished to get into the enclosure.

The crowded state of that soldiers' hut was beyond belief. The beds were arranged as closely as possible, and then another layer fixed on to the tops of the ground floor ones.

For the first three weeks of our life in this camp, we had to live mainly on the rations provided by the German authorities, since many of us had not been able to bring much in the way of tinned food along with us when we left Crefeld. The parcels from England were also delayed in their arrival, as the organization arranged for Crefeld had to be altered for Schwarmstedt. The food provided by the Germans at a daily cost to each officer of 1 mark 50 pfenning, comprised the following: *Breakfast*, coffee, of the war variety, probably made with acorns. *Dinner*, soup, always containing lumps of mangel-wurzel, cabbage, black peas, and occasional pieces of potato. Twice or three times a week, tiny shreds of real meat could be discovered in the soup. There was often a liberal ration of grit in this soup, but no extra charge was made on account of that. *The Evening Meal*, soup of the sago or meal variety, generally exceedingly thin.

In addition to these daily rations, we were each allowed to purchase two pounds of war bread per week at 60 pfs. This war bread was exceedingly nasty and doughy. If pressed with the finger the indentation remained, as it does in other putty-like substances.

Its color was a dark grey brown, and its smell and taste were sour. I understood that it was mainly made of potato. It is amusing to hear the talk about the English war bread in this country, to anyone who has experienced the same commodity in Germany.

The German war bread most certainly has violent effects on the interior economies of those who eat it for the first time, without becoming gradually trained to stand the strain of such an ordeal by eating the different grades of bread which have been given to the Fatherland during the last two years.

Personally I cannot justly complain, as I was one of the few who did not suffer from eating it.

It was a great day when the first consignment of re-directed parcels arrived. By standing in a queue for two hours the parcel could be obtained from the German censors. One of the first prisoners to draw his parcel came back with it under his arm, and a disgusted expression on his face. Nobody dared ask what he had got in his parcel, he looked too savage for the risk to be taken. However, it soon got about that he had got a dozen tennis balls! It was not surprising that he had looked like murder, when one realised that no tennis was possible in this camp, and that food was what he most wanted.

Fortunately our trials in this latter respect soon ended, as the parcels began to come in as regularly as they did at Crefeld. In addition the Crefeld commandant's promise, that the food boxes would be sent on, was fulfilled, and once more we had plenty of provisions. The soldiers also received their parcels now, and from what some of them said, they generally do wherever they are, thanks to the untiring energy of those who see to this for them in England.

One day we caught a specimen of the beasts which attacked us at night, and took it to the German officer pinned on a board. He made excuses and blamed the wooden huts, saying how impossible it was to deal with vermin. However, our room was to be fumigated. We were ordered to clear everything out of our room, and then the Germans arrived with a blow-flame with which to run over the bedsteads and clear out the cracks in the walls. Another German splashed creosote on to the floor, and places too high up to be reached by the blow flame.

We realized that this was all "eyewash," as the gaps between the partition walls separating the rooms were in some cases wide enough to allow the passage of one's hand. Therefore the many footed beasts of prey lurking in such places would easily avoid the strafing by going a few inches next door via these cracks. Of course the other rooms were not fumigated at the same time, so their preserves must have been entered by the game driven out of ours. We all wrote home for Keating's, but the letters never fetched up.

The censoring of our letters was done at a headquarter censor's office at Osnabrück, after our removal from Crefeld. This meant endless delay and often non-arrival of incoming letters, and practically a complete suspension of the outgoing mail.

The reason for this latter fact is not difficult to explain. Of course the prisoners described the new camp in these letters, and as the place was bad from every point of view, the contents of these epistles were not liked by the censors at Osnabrück. Consequently the letters were either burnt or kept. Of course the non-arrival of letters in England would do more to cause inquiries to be made at this end than anything else, but the Germans don't see things in that light.

This camp, Schwarmstedt, was known as No. 2, but why a number should be assigned and no name given to it, only a Boche could say; possibly it was because the Germans did not want it visited by any interfering inquisitive neutral country representative, since it was such a bad camp. I was pleased to hear that it was visited shortly after, and a full report made. I believe some of the grievances were attended to.

When we were at Crefeld some of us had taken up fencing as a form of exercise and amusement. The sabres and épées were sent out from England, but the Germans were very careful to take charge of them on their arrival, and used to let us have them at specific times, locking them up carefully at six o'clock every evening.

This care was continued for over a year, and then I suppose realising at last that as weapons with which to attack the camp-guards they were absolutely useless and that bed legs would be much more likely weapons if anyone wished to do such an absurd thing, they suddenly ignored the old fencing weapon and we were able each to have his own. When we moved from Crefeld, I took mine with me, tied quite openly on to a kit bag.

I hung it up in my room without thinking anything about it, until one day we were told that we were to be visited by a Boche General, and that everything had to be extremely tidy and in its correct place. As the authorities here were much more fussy persons than those at Crefeld, and the arriving general was rumoured a particularly aggressive England-hater, I thought that I had better hide my sabre, which I did almost entirely, only about three inches of it showing. Naturally I was a trifle worried about this compromising thing, as I had never realised before that it might get me into trouble in this new camp.

Whenever there was a search I had to hide it; in fact I got to dislike that sabre. I never got rid of it finally because I got rid of myself instead and left it behind as a legacy to my room companions. I hope they haven't claimed it and taken over its troublesome propensities.

At one end of the camp were three small huts known as machine-gun houses, constructed originally so as to command the three streets of the enclosure. In two of these the senior British officers lived, nine in a room.

The other one was the orderly room. In addition to these three houses, there were several machine-gun towers dotted at intervals outside but close up to the main wire fence of the camp.

These also must have been designed originally as points from which turbulent prisoners could be overawed. After a week or so of English occupation of this camp, one of them was cunningly used to give cover to an escaping party.

The exit from the camp was successful, but the actors in this drama were caught and brought back after several days away. The offending tower was promptly pulled down by the Germans and an extra sentry posted in its place.

Near the soldiers' quarters was the building assigned to "cells." I never saw the inside of them, but they were extremely small and hot in the summer. Officers in cells were marched out to the "bath" twice a week, and we could see them quite close, and sometimes even speak with them, while this was going on. They looked very white after a fortnight in these places, but that was due probably to the lack of sunlight. Each cell had a barred window about eight feet from the ground and occasionally we could see the faces of the occupants staring through the bars.

Another wooden hut did service as a hospital. This building was the best in the camp, being painted white on the inside and having quite a clean appearance. There were not many officer prisoners sick in this hospital when I left. Three or four bed cases was the total, on the average day.

Owing to the great heat, the rough grass and bog myrtle became extremely dry, and when a fire did break out it burnt merrily for a long time in the surrounding country.

On several occasions the flames swept down on the camp, and the German guards not on duty were turned out to prevent their too close approach to the wooden buildings.

Once a fire was only stopped ten yards short of the nearest hut.

The smoke was very thick and drove across the camp, obliterating it. Needless to say, some of us were watching the sentries very closely during this, but nobody got an opportunity of attacking the barbed wire perimeter by which we were enclosed. Rumour had it that a German village a few miles away had been wiped out by one of these fires. The German civilians of course blamed the prisoners, saying that they had caused these fires when smoking on parole-walks. The commandant then ordered no smoking except on roads, while we were out walking.

The German commandant of this camp full well realised what an extremely unpleasant place it was and how unsuited for the accommodation of officers or for private soldiers for that matter. Evidently ordered to make the best of a bad job, and told to try and smooth over the bad particulars of the camp by the skillful giving of small privileges, he attempted to get the prisoners interested in the building of a theatre and the making of playing-fields outside the camp.

A strong section of the prisoners fortunately hung together and declared themselves solidly against taking advantage of these privileges until such time as the really important questions, which had already been the subject of numerous complaints by the prisoners, should be attended to, and action for the general welfare of the camp population taken by the German authorities.

This camp was a miserable one if judged only from the details of existence there, but fortunately, as so often happens, there was a brighter side to it.

The uncomfortable and trying conditions made for unity and co-operation among the prisoners themselves. The humorous side of life seemed to come to the fore more easily than at the comparatively comfortable camp of Crefeld.

Cliques and factions existing during the previous two years at Crefeld were inclined to disappear, and a more general feeling of a common cause in the face of an unpleasant period steadily grew, closing the gaps in the ranks of the prisoners and tending to bring together people who would hardly bear to see each other under previous conditions.

It is surprising what a difference the effect of a long term of imprisonment has on various people. To anyone gifted with the smallest powers of observation, the constant changes and rapid transformation of ideas and standpoints in the small world of prison necessarily came with interest. It is a strange fact, but nevertheless true, that some prisoners, forgetting that a prison-existence is only temporary and entirely unnatural, seem to think that things matter in such a place, and that the happenings and views of the outside world do not directly concern them.

A long spell of such an existence changes a man more in character than the same period spent in the ordinary course of life. Some are tempered in the fires of such a test, while there are others....

PART II

CHAPTER IV

MY ESCAPE FROM THE CAMP

It may be wondered why it is that so few British officers have succeeded in escaping from prison camps in Germany.

The Germans do not get very worried over the loss of a few private soldiers in that way, but they are very careful to prevent our officers from having too many chances of escape.

The men are taken out to work in the fields and woods, and as the Germans have by no means too many men to spare, they cannot send a very large escort with them. Consequently it not unfrequently happens that men are able to slip away into thick cover without the Boches seeing them or knowing of their absence until they count up their charges, maybe some hours later.

The officers on the other hand never leave the barbed-wire enclosure of the camps, unless on parole for walks, an arrangement countenanced by our War Office, so they have naturally greater difficulties to get over before commencing any dash for the frontier.

Many officers have tried and have had appallingly bad luck in numerous instances. Early in the spring of 1917 the Germans warned all officers and men that they would be liable to five months and three months solitary confinement in a cell respectively, if caught attempting to escape. This was as a reprisal for excessive sentences inflicted on their prisoners who attempted to escape in England, under the Defence of the Realm Regulations.

As the solitary confinement was automatic, and was given without trial, we were also warned that after undergoing it, a transgressor of this kind might be tried by court-martial for such offences as being in possession of civilian clothes, a compass, German money, or wire-cutters, etc. The charge was simple.... Disobedience of orders! For this another three or four months could be imposed. I was very glad to read in the papers that all this sort of thing had been done away with by that excellent Commission which went to the Hague to meet the German delegates in July, 1917. There were other great things done by that same Commission, and the prisoners who benefit thereby will be most grateful.

Of course it was natural that with this heavy sentence hanging over the heads of would-be escapers some thought twice before trying, but it is worth noting that since this German order was issued there have been more successful escapes and more attempts to escape by officers than in the whole previous period.

I spoke to some of our men when out on a parole walk. They were working on a wild piece of heath-land with very few Germans to guard them. I asked one whether any of them had tried to escape from there. He told me that very few had done so, as there was such a long way to go, and that when caught the men were put in the cells and were not allowed their parcels.

This meant three-quarters starvation, as the German food provided was bad and scanty.

Our camp, known as Schwarmstedt, although situated seven or eight miles from the small town of that name, was on the Lüneburg Heide, an expanse of marshy, waste ground, intersected by small streams and dotted with little woods and stunted pine trees.

There were other camps on the same stretch of country. The notorious Soltau lay some miles to the north of our camp. This district is some hundred and seventy miles from the Dutch frontier as the crow flies.

In preparing my escape, I had to calculate the quantity of food required to carry me through the journey. This would naturally be considerable as I could not reckon on doing more than an average of eight to twelve miles every twenty-four hours, as it was only safe to march by night and the hours of darkness at that time of the year were only about five and a half. Although the actual distance was a hundred and forty-five miles, allowances to be made for detours and an indirect line, as well as for delays occasioned by such large obstacles as broad rivers and smaller, but more formidable ones in the shape of German guards, would necessitate preparations for a greater distance.

The food required would have to be carried, so a bag was necessary.

I will not say how I got the bag or what kind it was, nor how I got my civilian clothes, for this is certain to be read by members of the thorough race whose prisoner I was, and naturally any hints I drop may be used against other prisoners.

What I say outright is all known to the Germans, or obvious to the veriest fool of a prison-camp commandant.

My costume consisted of a long white cotton coat and a pair of white cotton pants, both dyed a dirty light grey-brown with coffee. I had a cap also, but that too must remain a mystery.

As the cotton coat had no pockets and was very thin, I wore an old khaki coat underneath, which stood me in good stead when I had nearly got to the end of my journey. A pair of rubber-soled shoes, white once but made khaki-colour by my servant some time before, completed my kit.

Although I had naturally discussed matters with others in the camp in an indefinite way I had not arranged any collaboration in the scheme, by which I succeeded. I told only one friend ten minutes before I took the first steps in the carrying out of the plan.

When first we reached Schwarmstedt after our journey from Crefeld, there were several weak spots in the "ring" of precautions against escape which surrounded it. Within forty-eight hours of our arrival three officers got out of the camp.

They had very bad luck, being caught after eleven days' travel, about three-quarters of the way to the Dutch frontier. This loophole was of course closed to further attempts by the measures now adopted by the Boches.

However, two more got away from the camp not long afterwards and had the same atrocious luck after going about the same distance. Another individual attempt resulted in an officer getting out for some days before the same Nemesis overtook him, and he too was brought back.

About ten days before my escape, yet two more got away, and were still unaccounted for when I left the camp. They must have had the same hard fate, as I heard nothing of them in Holland or England when I arrived. After each of these attempts the Germans discovered fresh weak spots, and the camp was rapidly becoming a stronger prison. One effect they had was to make the Germans employ more guards for the camp. Extra sentries were put on at several places, and every extra sentry means reliefs, and it takes six men at least to permanently provide one extra sentry.

These men might have been helping on the farms instead, so it is some small comfort to think that even a failure to escape can do some service to our country.

Of course when I left most of these unfortunates were back in the cells, beginning their five months' stretch of solitary confinement.

Anyone looking at the map of Germany will see immediately that from the Lüneburg Heide, north of Hanover, one has to cross the following rivers before one can reach the Dutch frontier—the Aller, Leine, Weser, Hunte and Ems.

These are all fairly large. The Aller runs along the western limits of the Lüneburg Heide (Heath) and acts as a natural barrier around prison-camps situated to the east of it. When we first arrived at this camp, Schwarmstedt, the commandant had practically told us in so many words that we might get away from the camp, but that we should never cross the frontier. This meant that there was something which he knew of to be passed besides the camp guards and those at the frontier. Many of us promptly understood by his remarks that he had himself made arrangements for the guarding of the bridges over the rivers.

Another fact generally well-known to every one is this. All bridges over large important rivers are guarded in Germany, and even the railway bridges over many of the smaller ones are provided with their ancient Landsturm men.

On our arrival the commandant of our camp had spoken at once to us in English, of which he knew a certain amount. We soon got to see how proud of this knowledge he was, as he would address all the English officers on some trifling subject every second day. Besides which he would summon the senior English officer before him and all those officers who had any particular department of the camp to look after, such as kitchens, parcels, games, practically every day. The language spoken was always English.

He was a fine-looking old man, covered with medals and iron crosses, a veteran of the 1866 and 1870 wars. He loved being saluted, and complained that the British did not salute him enough. He was told that our officers do not salute when they are not wearing hats, and that many had got no military caps since theirs had been taken from them by the Germans at the time of their capture.

SECTION OF A GERMAN CAMP

He promptly ordered the canteen to get caps and sell them to us. When they arrived they were very comic to look at, dark blue with a stiff peak.

Before describing my actual exit from the camp it is necessary that the general plan of the enclosure and its adjacent buildings be understood.

The camp was oblong in shape, and was surrounded on all sides by a barbed-wire fence some eleven feet high. At every fifty yards there was posted a sentry, whose orders included the shooting of any hapless wretch found cutting his way through the fence, or climbing over it. Opposite one of the corners of the camp, and outside of it, was situated the parcel office. Here the prisoners' parcels were censored by the Germans in front of them.

There was also a tin office here, where all tinned food not immediately required by the prisoners was kept until it was needed, when it could be taken away after being opened by a German. We often used to try and make the German soldier jump by saying "Bomben" or "Handgranaten" just at the moment when he punctured the tin with his opener.

These two offices were open until 6 o'clock in the evening, and the Germans had put up a barbed-wire passage from a gate in the wire wall of the camp enclosure to the door of this office, thus enabling them to permit the prisoners free access to these two rooms until this hour. At 6 o'clock the offices were cleared of prisoners by the numerous Germans employed there and cut off from the prisoners' part of the camp by closing the iron gate in the main wire wall of the camp.

It occurred to me that if I could hide in the parcel office or tin room before 6 o'clock, and be locked in when the work of the day ceased, I should naturally find myself outside the wire enclosure, which was the first and principal difficulty to be overcome by a would-be escaper.

It would then remain to be seen whether it was feasible to get out of these offices by way of the skylights or other windows at a late hour.

The risk was worth taking, but another difficulty presented itself. How was I to get my pack, full of food, boots, civilian clothes, etc., and all the rest of my paraphernalia, weighing fully fifty pounds, into the parcel office without making the numerous

Germans I should have to pass suspicious. The solution to this question came two days after I was ready.

At about 5.30 p.m. on Tuesday, June 19th, a tremendous wind came down on the camp, and the sandy dust rose in a huge cloud filling everybody's eyes, noses, and mouths with fine particles.

This seemed to me a good opportunity, and I quickly put my pack into a large wooden box, nailed down the lid, and carried it to the parcel office.

The Germans were far too busy thinking about the dust in their eyes to wonder why a box was being carried into the parcel-office, whereas boxes were always carried "away" from there. I passed several Germans without any trouble and got into the tin room, where I deposited the box on the floor. I now had twenty minutes in which to hide. While pretending to be extremely interested in what I was going to have for my meal that evening, I looked round, and saw at once that the best hiding-place without doubt was on the top of the pigeon holes in which everybody kept their tins. These pigeon-holes, about two feet square and two and a half feet deep, were made of wood and were ranged along each wall, tier above tier for about twelve to fourteen feet. There was a ledge at the top about two feet below the level of the roof. I decided to get up onto that ledge, knowing full well that nobody looks round a room at a much higher level than his own eyes, and that a hungry German gaze would never wander farther than the level of the nearest food.

This was a good start, but unfortunately there was a Boche painting numbers on the lockers within six feet of the spot from which I should have to climb up to my hiding-place. However, he did not look intelligent, wore spectacles, and was very engrossed in his work, so I thought I could risk his not seeing me. I had rubber shoes on, my boots being in the bag, so I was not afraid on the score of noise.

I was lucky in choosing the right moment, and succeeded in climbing slowly and quietly up and then putting myself into a lying position along the ledge without either the Boche or three other English officers getting out tins near by, being aware that anything strange had happened.

I lay there hardly daring to breathe, with four slats of wood fixed cross-ways in a vertical position, so that the sharp edges were uppermost, catching me at various unprotected and tender points of my body and legs. However, it did not last for ever. The officers left, and no more came in; and then the German soldier packed up his tools.

He left, and very shortly afterwards in came the under-officer in charge. He looked at the windows, walked round the office and then, quickly slipping a tin from a handy pigeon-hole into his pocket, left the room, locking the door after him.

I was locked in and was able to breathe again.

After giving my pilfering friend another twenty minutes in case he should have under-estimated his appetite and should return for more, I got down and rubbed my cramped legs. This done I had a meal and then settled myself down to wait till 11 o'clock, which I deemed the earliest hour for commencing operations with safety.

The skylights appeared to be the best exit from the room, and under one of them there was a convenient beam. The other skylight proved to be out of reach of anything.

Since the building was of wood, I had to exercise great caution in moving about, so creaky were the boards. At 11 o'clock I climbed up to the beam and then crawled along it till I was exactly under my skylight. Then getting my shoulders well under it I heaved. Horror of horrors; it gave an awful crack and would not budge a hair's-breadth. This was a nuisance, only I called it something stronger than that! I got down, afraid that the loud crack must have alarmed the sentries, two of whose beats joined exactly opposite this tin room. However I was able to thank my good luck again as they had heard nothing. I had now to find another way out. I tried unpicking the lock with a bent nail, but had no success. I then tried to take the screws out of the lock with a table knife. One came loose but the others refused to shift at all. Foiled here I tried the wooden partition between the tin room and the passage beyond; but again I could make no progress, as the carpenters had done their work too well. I sat down on my box and sweated. The atmosphere of this closed room was simply appalling and my clothes were wringing wet by reason of it. It looked now as if I should be found next morning in this office, and get five months' solitary confinement in the cells for trying to escape, and not even have a run for my money. There still remained one chance, the most dangerous and therefore left until desperation should drive me to it. The side windows of the tin-office, some three and a half feet from the floor, opened onto the sentry's beat, exactly opposite the point where the other sentry, whose beat ran at right angles to the office, joined in. In addition there was a large arc lamp within thirty feet of these windows. My idea now was to watch until both sentries should be walking down their beats away from me, and therefore naturally with their backs turned, and then open my window, jump out, and run for it.

The windows were made in two halves hinging at the sides and opening outwards.

I could always get the sentry opposite the window walking in the right direction as a beginning. I had then to open the right-half of the window three or four inches in order to see where the other sentry was, as he walked up and down parallel to the windows and close up against the building. Of course I was in mortal dread each time I opened my window to find out his position, of discovering myself looking straight into his face. I never got such a bad shock as that, but neither did I ever get the two of them walking with their backs turned at the same time.

Wednesday, 20th June. I had to shut the window every time I saw that he was approaching, as he was certain to see it when he came close if I left it open. Nine times I tried this experiment and had no luck. I then sat down to think for a bit. Fortunately I remembered now that the sentries were changed at 2.30 a.m., so I thought that I would try to turn this fact to my advantage. Sentry changing consisted of twelve Germans in file marching round the camp, clock-wise, picking up the old sentry and dropping the new one.

I hoped that the noise caused by their heavy boots would drown all noise made by me, and that this crowd of men rounding the corner and marching towards my most difficult sentry would hide me from him. It happened just as I hoped. They relieved the sentry opposite my window well down his beat and he stood still, as they always do for a minute or two after being newly posted.

Then on came the twelve Landsturm-men, rounded the corner, making a fine noise and dust with their heavy boots. When the last of them was about fifteen yards from my window, and all twelve were strung out between it and the difficult sentry, I pushed open both halves of the window, pitched out my heavy pack, which fell with a thud, and jumped out after it. To pick it up, jump into the ditch, run along the path, and round the corner away from the dazzling rays of the arc lamp did not take many seconds. I was out. I listened for the excitement which would tell of the discovery of my flight, but all was quiet, so I was able to steal off in a westerly direction.

CHAPTER V

CROSSING THE FIRST TWO RIVERS

After walking steadily away from the camp in a westerly direction for about a mile and a half, I found running water which was a God-send. Here I filled my water bottle (an empty wine bottle bound round with cloth and string) and had a good drink.

Pushing on to the south-west I continued along a rough track running through marshy ground. By this time the dawn had spread its light sufficiently to make objects clear a long way ahead. From the marshy ground rose the cries of curlews and peewits,—the drumming of snipe and the hoarse croakings of many frogs making an unearthly tout ensemble. It was a strange feeling to be out and walking freely along this quiet track, and the mist which hung about the ground on either side of the road gave a weird shape to everything. For the first time I was able to think of other things than the details of escape, and I counted up my chances. At any rate I had got out, and if I were caught I should at least have made a determined effort and would be able to feel I had done my duty in attempting.

After an hour's walking I left the marshy country behind and struck woods and clumps of young pine trees. At last at about 4.30 a.m. I approached a metalled road which ran across my front. I advanced cautiously to the edge of it and then heard German voices. Some boys and women were milking and tending cattle not far away.

Thinking that to move forward at this hour, which is always one of the most active in the day with the hard-working farmers of Germany, would be to risk detection, I decided to rest where I was in hiding. I found a thick clump of young firs within sixty yards of the road and deposited my lumpy bag down in a place where the moss was thick and soft. A drink of water followed by a few biscuits and a piece of chocolate, sufficed for a meal, and then I lay down and tried to sleep, which I found impossible to do, although I was tired enough.

It was bitterly cold lying still, and my clothes, wringing wet with perspiration as they were, clung to me and took away all natural warmth.

I suppose I got an hour's sleep before 11 o'clock, when it got so hot that it became quite unpleasant in my hiding-place. These hours passed very slowly and I felt the need of someone with whom to talk. At 3 o'clock I thought I would move forward and try to get up to the bank of the river without being seen. After crossing the road I proceeded for half a mile or so before leaving the thick cover which was plentiful hereabouts and got into a grove of large trees at the side of a field. Now I discovered that any further advance was out of the question at that time, as all the fields in front of me were hay-fields in the process of being cut, and I could see fourteen or fifteen Germans working at the cutting. I stayed where I was until about eight o'clock, when I saw that most of the workers had left the fields and gone home. I pushed on a bit now, making a detour to the north, and soon saw the main road bridge over the river.

By watching this I came to the conclusion that it had no guard posted on it, at any rate by day, but many civilians were walking across, and a hay cart passed every minute or so.

Pushing on again I crossed the main road and got into the thick cover to the north of it and close to the river. As I was filthily dirty from the dust storm I thought I would bathe at a safe spot well away from the bridge, deciding to post myself in the bushes close up to it as soon as it became dusk. The bathe passed off without incident, and after all, as it struck me while I was swimming about, what better disguise could I have than nakedness. If anyone came along I could act the German very thoroughly, knowing enough of the language to answer any question while swimming. The bathe was delightful and refreshed me exceedingly. After dressing I found that it was practically dark, so set off for my hiding-place close to the bridge. I got safely to it and lay down in a ditch running through some bushes within ten yards of the beginning of the wooden structure.

My plan was to cross as soon as it became quite dark.

I had been there scarcely ten minutes when I saw two German women come out of the house at the other end of the bridge and cross over towards me, followed at some thirty yards by a German soldier. He caught them up just opposite me and all three, talking hard, went some forty yards along the road, and then sat down in the bushes on my side of it. Here they were soon joined by another soldier who came from the direction of the camp, as I discovered on hearing his voice. I was now so placed that I was actually between them and the bridge, but dared not move, as I was certain to make the bushes surrounding my hiding-place rustle and the dead sticks lying about crack. I waited in hopes that they would go away, but it got quite dark and still the giggles of the women and the low tones of the men continued.

"AT LAST THE TWO WOMEN GOT UP"

At last, at about 11 o'clock, the two women got up, and after standing talking for a few minutes I heard one of them say to the men, "You must now remain quite quiet! Nicht?" And they answered yes, and I heard them all say good-night and the women walked back along the road across the bridge and went into their own house, leaving the two men still in the bushes. I waited for them to go also, but they did not budge. A silence as of the dead came over everything, and I knew then that they were an ambush, and a very cunningly placed one too. Naturally, anyone looking to see if a bridge was guarded or not would expect to find the sentries on the middle or at either end of the bridge itself and could then clear away from the place if it proved to be unhealthy. However, this ambush was placed so as to catch any wretch moving cautiously along the side of the road, straining his eyes eagerly forward to see if the near end of the bridge was or was not guarded, little thinking as he did so of any cunning ambush fifty to sixty yards away from the bridge itself.

Thursday, 21st June. I now set myself to tire the Germans out by waiting, and hoped that in the early hours of the morning they would be less alert than usual.

I lay there, bitten all over by mosquitos, and having a very uncomfortable time of it. I heard one of them cough, and then, after an hour or two of silence, another cough. Altogether I waited about four hours, and it was not till roughly three o'clock that I thought I could risk a move.

Very cautiously I now began to crawl on all-fours towards the road, carefully feeling all the ground as I did so in order to be able to remove the dead sticks lying across my track. By pushing through the bushes very slowly I avoided making much of a noise and gained the embankment along the top of which ran the road, without causing any suspicion. Here I had a breather and then continued my crawl upwards. I reached the top of the bank which was the edge of the road, and, knowing that I was well against the sky-line to the eyes of watchers below, did not waste much time before turning towards the bridge, and keeping well down, crawled steadily onwards, reducing the space of time in which I risked being seen very rapidly. Another fifty yards on all fours and I ventured to get on to my feet and walk, in my rubber-soled shoes. Fifty yards more and I was safely off the planking of the bridge and on to the road proper with plenty of cover all round me.

As my clothes were of a light coffee tint they assimilated very well with the colours of the dusty road and the white painted woodwork of the bridge.

I felt inclined to roar with laughter at the ambush after gaining the far side of the river, and would dearly have loved to have shouted insults and gibes back at them, instead of which I continued my walk quietly along the road, keeping well to one side under the trees which so often border country roads in Germany. I soon came to a village, and feeling that this one was too close to the bridge, which had been guarded, to require anything for itself in this line, walked through it without even causing a dog to bark. I continued for an hour before anything else happened, and then I very nearly made a bad error. I was sleepy I suppose and was not so sharp on the look-out as I ought to have been, and I suddenly got an awful shock on distinctly seeing in front of me in the first light of the dawn two men in dark clothes approaching. I immediately turned about and walked away from them as hard as I could go. Gaining on them rapidly I continued till they were too far behind to be seen and then jumped into the corn on the right of the road, and after running fifty yards into it, lay still. Sure enough these two men had slowly continued their walk and now passed me, carrying on for a hundred yards before they also stopped. Thinking that it was time to be off, especially as it was getting lighter every moment, I took a detour through the corn-fields and striking the road about half a mile further on crossed it and took a turn in the corn on the other side. Then after about a mile of making winding tracks through their precious wheat, rye and barley crops, I again struck the road and hurried along it to make up for lost time.

This wandering about I considered necessary in order to delay and perhaps bamboozle any police dog put on my track. I had no doubt that these two men were policemen and that they had only just caught a glimpse of me which had made them curious. I am certain I again had to thank my whitish suit for my immunity from determined pursuit.

After this little excitement I had to move very rapidly as it was already nearly daylight, and I wished to get to the banks of the next river before hiding.

Pushing along the road I struck a small town, and crossed the end of it, taking a level crossing on the way. Seeing nobody at the station near-by I gained more confidence again, and was not so upset as I might have been when I found that I had to walk for a mile or more along a road flanked on both sides with houses.

At last and by no means too soon I got to the river bank, had a drink, refilled my water-bottle and set about looking for a hiding-place in which to sleep during the day. This river, the Leine, is about seventy yards broad and is deep and fairly sluggish. There was a bridge crossing it about a mile downstream from the place at which I drank.

I found a hiding-place not far from the river, but after a short while I began to think that it was a bad one, as although in this district most of the hay had been cut, one field quite near had still to be done. So off I went to look for a better place. I found a thick hedge which looked likely, and then suddenly saw a girl bathing eighty yards away. However, I quickly decided that she could never have seen me, and began to pull aside some brambles with a view to getting in. Suddenly without any warning I heard just behind me "Guten Morgen." I turned in a second and found myself face to face with a flapper dressed all in white, on her way to bathe.

I growled back "Good Morning" and she passed on. I expect she also got a shock, for I must have been a wild-looking object. I decided now that this was no place for me and began to make tracks as soon as she had moved away. I hadn't gone a hundred yards when I heard a man's voice and the yapping of a dog come from where I had spoken to the flapper. He was speaking to the girls, so fearing that my girl might have mentioned seeing an extraordinary apparition on her way, and so arouse suspicions in the mind of the man, I cleared out and went through the woods, which were fairly thick here for about a mile.

I was lucky now to find a deserted factory quite close to the bridge which I had seen previously. By this factory was a thick patch of small fir trees, into which I forced my way and found excellent cover among the dense undergrowth and lower branches of the trees. I tried to sleep, but had little success, and was again worried by flies and heat at about midday. My watch had stopped, so I arranged some sticks so that when their shadow pointed north by my compass I should know it was roughly noon, and be able to set my watch.

I was keeping a collection of hieroglyphics which I cannot honour with the title of "Diary." I purposely made it unreadable, and abbreviated all the words so that it would convey nothing to the Boche if they caught me.

Unless one keeps some sort of record it is very easy to forget the day of the week, etc., and that is necessary knowledge, as Sunday is a special day in Germany and must be treated differently by an escapee.

It had become very uncomfortable in my hiding-place and sleep was out of the question for some reason, so I thought that as I had lost time already by being delayed both nights, I must try to make up for the delay, and what would help to do so more than anything else would be the crossing of the Leine by daylight. The more I thought of it the more I wished to get that river behind me as soon as possible. I decided that at any rate I would scout the bridge and then make up my mind.

This proved easier than I had hoped, because I found that the bridge had no cover anywhere near it, so that I was able to see without any trouble from quite a distance away that there was no sentry on the bridge or in the neighbourhood. There being no cover, ambushes were out of the question. I thought then that I might easily cross at once, as at night there was always the possibility of finding that a sentry had been posted simply for the hours of darkness, those being the hours during which prisoners generally move, a fact that the Germans know well.

Accordingly I got on to the road and walked boldly along it, reading a German newspaper which I had found and kept the day before.

Just before reaching the bridge I met a very nice-looking German girl carrying two pails of milk. She deigned to honour me, tramp though I looked, with a sweet smile and a most encouraging "good-day." I suppose the shortage of young men in the Fatherland was accountable for this; it would hardly have been due to my personal beauty. However, she didn't meet with much response beyond a surly "good-day" from behind my newspaper. On the bridge itself I met an older woman who just looked at me and didn't answer my good-day. That made me hurry on somewhat. I got across without any trouble and didn't see a sign of a sentry, and I was not surprised at that, seeing how near the Aller and Leine are to each other.

It would mean many more men called away from farm work to arrange for the guarding of the crossings of the Leine as well; a fact which hardly recommends itself to the Boche authorities just at present.

CHAPTER VI

I MEET FOX AND BLANK

The fact that this bridge was left behind made me feel quite elated, and I continued along a lane in a westerly direction with full confidence in my disguise and my evidently unsuspicious appearance generally.

The lane ending in a field made me take to working across country. There were quite a number of Germans scattered about making hay. I had to go very cautiously so as to avoid meeting anyone face to face, as they might have asked me awkward questions relating to my work, etc. I also could not walk across fields with long grass in them by day without risking causing suspicions in the minds of any farmer who might see me, as the Germans themselves are very careful not to damage any crops in these times.

And now happened the most remarkable thing that could well have fallen to the experience of anyone outside a novel.

I was walking along a hedge very slowly, watching a German in the distance, when suddenly I thought I heard my name being spoken very clearly and distinctly. Again I heard it and this time I was certain, and immediately thought that I was imagining it and that I was really going mad. I was told afterwards that I clutched my head with both hands. It was an awful shock to hear this, after not having seen anyone or been with anyone who knew me for two and a half days, and having crossed two rivers and got miles from the camp in which my only acquaintances and friends in Germany were locked up. I turned round and then I heard it again coming out of the hedge, and not only my name this time but an exceedingly English sentence which told me that I was a something fool, and that I was to come back. I promptly did so and found Major C.V. Fox, D.S.O., and Lieut. Blank lying at the bottom of the hedge. I at once joined them, and I naturally thought that all the officers from the camp had escaped and were spread far and wide over Germany, and that I had found a couple of them without being unduly lucky. However, that was not the case. Fox and Blank had escaped sixteen hours after I did, but while I had been hung up between the ambush and the first bridge for four hours, they had pushed ahead and crossed both rivers and got to their present hiding-place at daybreak.

It was a great relief to have somebody with whom to talk, and we set to and discussed details in low whispers.

I then found out that I had not been missed at roll-call the night I had hidden in the tin office.

Fox told me his adventures and I gave him an account of mine in exchange.

Again our luck was well to the fore. On examining our supplies of food, etc., I found that Fox had lost nearly all his biscuits and chocolate in the crossing of the Aller, which they had had to negotiate by swimming a raft across. This had got swamped, as its buoyancy was poor, naturally with disastrous consequences to much of the perishable food they had taken with them.

I had got a good number, and so would be able to supply them and in exchange they gave me other things.

My compass was a good one, theirs poor; whereas my map was exceedingly bad and theirs quite good.

We found that we had both the same ideas of the route to be taken towards the frontier. The Germans had captured three other lots of escapers in the district around Osnabrück.

Forest guards were active in the woods in this district, and this had decided both of us on our line before we met.

Another fact which made us the more sure which route we should follow was the nature of the ground as shown by the maps. The country which we eventually traversed is shown as marshy, and we had both decided that the great drought in Germany this summer would have dried this up to a very large extent, and we hoped that the Germans might not have taken this fact into consideration in allocating guards, so that this district would be more lightly watched than others. As a matter of fact the maps exaggerate the marshes, and I should think that even after really wet weather it would be possible to follow the same line.

"FACE TO FACE WITH A FLAPPER
ON HER WAY TO BATHE"

The one disadvantage to this joining-up of parties lay in its greater visibility and the loss of its elasticity, owing to the fact that we were now three whereas two is the ideal number. It is naturally more difficult for three to dive into hiding immediately on sighting a German than it is for one or two.

However, the pros easily outweighed the cons. While we were thus talking we got rather a scare. A man on a horse came along the road and stopped immediately opposite the patch of brambles in the midst of which we lay. The horse began tearing at the leaves of a small tree, thereby making a noise which seemed to us, cowering under cover, as if it might be caused by the man trying to force his way into our hiding-place.

We lay absolutely still, but we felt very uncomfortable, especially as the contents of our bags were mostly strewn about the ground drying. We should never have had time to collect our belongings together and bolt if an intrusion resulted in our hiding-place being exposed. However, after two or three minutes of suspense on our part the horse moved on down the road and we breathed again.

Up to this time I had been exceedingly sparing in what I had eaten. In fact I had overdone my economy in this respect, as I had felt a bit weak once or twice that day. The other two had fed well up till then, and when I saw what they intended to eat that evening I also increased my ration. From this time onwards we usually had a pound of food each per day.

This we intended to augment when possible.

The details of Fox and his companion's adventures are outside the scope of this narrative, but the broad facts which must be included in order to account for their presence in the hedge are as follows.

On Wednesday afternoon, 20th June, they had left Schwarmstedt camp with a fatigue party detailed for tree-felling, disguised as British soldiers. The Germans of course did not realise that two of the party were really officers, but they were naturally bound to find out the deception which had been practised on them on the return of the fatigue party to camp. The fatigue party broke up and scattered about while working at their tree-felling job, and it was not possible for the German escort to keep a watch on all and every soldier at the same time.

Accordingly these two, nicely judging their chance, slipped away when the Boches were looking in the other direction.

It did not take them long to get some distance away, and that night they approached the river Aller with the object of effecting a crossing.

On nearing the railway bridge they had discovered an ambush waiting for them, and consequently cleared away from that area.

Striking the river some distance up-stream, they made a rough raft from wooden palings, and putting their food and clothes on it swam it across. It was here that Fox discovered that his companion was far from being a strong swimmer. Therefore

Fox, who had not entirely recovered from the injuries he had received in a previous attempt to escape by jumping from a train, had to swim the raft backwards and forwards several times by himself until all the food and clothing had been transported across. The raft was not a large one or very buoyant, which resulted in much of the food being destroyed. Fox also assisted Blank to cross, so had plenty of swimming to do.

After crossing this river, they had pushed rapidly on and crossed another by a bridge, without apparently getting into any trouble.

They reached their hiding-place during the early hours of Thursday morning and had remained there all day, drying their goods and chattels.

CHAPTER VII

THE CROSSING OF THE WESER

We had decided to begin the night's march at 10 o'clock should it be possible to do so. When we started it was not far off that hour, and in consequence was still fairly light.

As there was an old well in the field at the side of which we had been hidden all day, we went to it in hopes of finding water. This we were fortunate enough to get. It was the kind of water that would only be drunk by cattle and escaped prisoners.

After filling our water bottles we commenced our march westwards. Very soon we struck a rather wild stretch of country and were startled by the sight of fireworks not far from us. After various rockets and Roman candles had fizzled themselves out, we came to the conclusion that this display constituted no additional risk to us, and pushed ahead. This stretch of rough country began to take a slope, and not long after we began the ascent of this incline we debouched on to an open plain. The weather had begun to look threatening about half an hour previously. Now it was clear to us that we were in for a wetting.

Striking westwards across this plateau we soon got into difficulties. Parts of it were decidedly boggy even after the great drought. Several streams and dykes intersected the country and barbed-wire fences were common and difficult to climb.

We had covered about four miles since our start, when suddenly the rain began to descend. Mutterings of thunder and odd flickers of lightning in the west boded ill for the coming hours. Soon the rain, which had begun falling fairly gently, increased its unwelcome efforts.

The thunderstorm very quickly established itself right over our heads and lightning flashed every second or so. It had got exceedingly dark, and in addition the rain, now descending in torrents, had made the hitherto dry ground into a morass. We were absolutely unable to make headway in the inky blackness which now reigned, so we got under some thick trees and sat down. These trees did not shelter us much, and it was not long before we were all soaked to the skin and shivering from head to foot. It was an ideal moment for discussing our future and its chances, and we did it, in a thoroughly depressed and miserable way. We quite envied our late companions their warm if hard apologies for beds at Schwarmstedt. However, all things have an end, and the rain eventually ceased and the darkness lifted somewhat.

Owing to the sodden state of the ground now the swampy bits had become really things of awe-inspiring proportions, which made us return eastwards for a mile or so in search of a road or track along which we could travel in the right direction. This we found and took, doing some three miles or so before the storm returned once more and we were again handicapped by the darkness. So dark was it in fact that we never noticed a bend in the road, and we continued in the same direction only to walk slap into a ditch bristling with barbed-wire. This decided us to halt again for a time. The same misery repeated itself, but this time tired nature asserted itself in the case of Blank, who slept like a log in the soaking ditch. We waited in this pretty state till the grey light of dawn gave us sufficient seeing-power to enable us to continue without risk of falling into ditches.

Friday, 22nd June. We naturally put on the pace after all this delay, and we soon got warm from hard walking.

Passing through a village and striking across country afterwards for lack of a track to follow, we hit a small river. This we waded through and got to rough heath country on the other side.

It was drizzling at intervals now, and we very much wished to find a dry and sheltered spot in which to lie up during the day.

We thought we had found something suitable in this line and called a halt at a dense clump of bushes and undergrowth of all kinds. We were disappointed in our place very soon, as the rain came through freely. After boiling some water and drinking the coffee we made with it, we decided to continue our trek, reasoning that an atrocious day like this would effectually keep early risers in-doors until a later hour at any rate. We were right in our conjecture, as, although we walked along the roads which are not safe places at 6 o'clock in the morning, we neither saw anyone nor any tracks in the mud which abounded everywhere.

Striking more north-west after an hour or so, we again hit a wild trackless moor. This we began to cross and soon came upon peat-cuttings.

Shortly after this we spied three huts. These at first interested and then fascinated us. At last, plucking up courage, we examined them. Their dry interiors and the lack of all traces of recent visits from human beings, decided us to do rather a risky thing, namely, to use them. Having begun risking we went the whole way and made a wood fire in the huts, from splinters torn from the benches, etc. Drying our clothes and cooking hot food of the oxo variety occupied considerable time. We took it in turns to sleep on the floor. This involved practically lying in the fire, but it had the advantage of allowing one to become thoroughly warm. There was a pond of excellent water by the hut we had chosen, so we had quite a number of drinks of coffee and beef tea, etc.

In the afternoon the sun came out to cheer us up a bit, but the scudding clouds did not give us much hope of a dry night. We intended to start at 10 o'clock, all being well. At about six I was suddenly taken ill, and for half an hour or so felt extremely miserable. I suppose it was a chill I had got, but fortunately it passed off fairly soon and I was able to eat and have some oxo two hours later. At ten o'clock we actually did start, but we were unfortunate in having pitch-darkness again in which to negotiate extremely difficult ground, as it had set in to rain once more in a thoroughly steady, lasting manner.

We had a bad fright over my compass—the best one. When I was ill the compass must have fallen out of my pocket, and although we searched diligently everywhere, it was only by the merest chance that I saw a piece of it showing up in the heather in which it was lost. Truly, a marvellous stroke of luck.

We had done about an hour's hard work ploughing through the rough boggy land, when we decided that we had better return to our hut once more, and tackle the bog next morning.

This delay meant that we should lose the night's march, a serious affair when food reserves are limited and long distances remain to be covered. However, the night's rest we got as the result of this delay was extremely valuable as a matter of fact, as we woke up in a much fresher state after sleeping till 7 a.m.

Saturday, 23rd June. Comfortably smoking our pipes in the dry warmth of our hut, after a breakfast of tinned beef, biscuit, and hot oxo, we were able to look on the bright side of things, and our fears on the subject of the crossing of the river Weser, to be undertaken within the next twenty-four hours, dwindled in strength until we were able to imagine it a trifling obstacle. We intended to make a raft and swim it over, should no boat be forthcoming during a short search.

While we were discussing these and sundry other matters, Fox suddenly saw two men in dark clothes running across the heath some thousand yards away from us. Who could they be? On they ran, one about thirty yards behind the other, until they both disappeared into a clump of stunted pine trees.

After a minute or two's discussion we agreed that probably they were also escaped prisoners.

If so, from what were they running? This question was answered shortly afterwards. A cart driven by two men suddenly came into sight not very far from the place where we had first seen the two running men.

This cart was coming towards our hut, and soon began to fill us with something stronger than mere interest in its movements.

It came to within 150 yards of us and then stopped. The men got out and began filling the cart with peat from the piles of this commodity lying about.

We by this time were lying on the bottom of the hut, or squashed up against the back of the door, not daring to move. We prayed that it would not come on to rain heavily, as the men would be certain then to take shelter in one of the huts, and ours was the nearest to them. This suspense continued for about half an hour, and then, with the cart filled, the two men departed the way they had come.

At about noon we made up our minds that we could safely attempt the crossing of the moor by day. Accordingly, after clearing the hut of all traces of our occupation we packed up our kit, shouldered our packs and set off. We had torn up the benches and taken planks off the back of one of the other huts, intending to carry them with us to serve as material for our raft for the crossing of the Weser, but now that we actually began our march we found that the weight of all this wood was very considerable and so at the last moment left the whole lot behind. We were fortunate in so doing, as the distance was much greater than we had realised, and, as it turned out, it would have been a case of carrying coals to Newcastle.

We proceeded to negotiate the same ground as that which we had attempted to cross and failed over the night before, and now realised how impossible a task it would have been in the inky blackness of the night, proving as it did a sufficiently difficult task even by daylight.

Two or three miles of boggy rough ground had to be covered, and during the last few hundred yards of this, before we reached the lowest slopes of a range of hills, we were continually going through the spongy soil up to our knees.

Fox, who was brought up amidst Irish bogs, chose the line, and we followed as nearly in his tracks as we possibly could. We were not sorry to get off this bit of difficult country, and we wondered what would have happened if we had continued our attempt the night before.

The range of hills we had now reached ran in a westerly direction for a few miles before sloping down to the valley of the Weser. They were covered with fine pine and fir woods, cut up every now and then into squares by drives made through them.

We saw several deer, and the additional presence of things that looked like shooting butts made us think that this area was probably some special deer-forest. None of us felt very safe, as deer-forests mean forest-guards. The lack of food in Germany has probably increased the numbers of the poaching fraternity, and the German authorities are sure not to have reduced the establishment of forest-guards. These ideas caused us usually to feel very nervous in woods, fine cover though they afford.

By 3 o'clock we had reached the western end of these hills and were able to look out over the Weser valley. Our enjoyment of the scenery was cut short by our hearing children's voices not far behind us. We bolted into cover like scared rabbits. The place we chose was a very thick plantation of young fir-trees. The shelter given us by this was excellent and we afterwards endeavoured to find similar places for our daily rests.

It had become pleasantly warm by now so we all got a little sleep and were very comfortable till about 8 o'clock, when it got cold and we naturally became anxious to move on again. I entered up my rough diary, and we found that we had little reason to be pleased at the pace at which we had travelled up to then.

Fox's right heel and my left ankle had got rubbed a day or so before, and by now had begun to get really troublesome. Providentially we had with us a small tin of boracic ointment with which we plastered these sore places every daily halt. At this halting-place we had a thorough overhaul of our possessions, and I mended my pack with string, as the great weight of its contents had begun to tell on its seams.

The children's voices continued to make themselves heard all round us, and one was forced to wonder what they found to scream and shout at for such hours on end. Of course Germany is the land of children, they are much more important in that country it appears than elsewhere. The grown-ups seem to understand them better, and certainly the kids themselves always seem to be extremely happy. This particular batch of brats was just playing in the woods I suppose, but their laughter and shouts caused us some alarm at first, until we got accustomed to the noise.

At about 9 p.m. we decided to commence our march, as we were particularly desirous of striking the Weser bank as soon as possible after complete darkness set in.

Pushing forward through thick undergrowth we had travelled some distance westwards, when we were forced to halt while several military wagons passed along a road a short distance in front of us. After they had left our immediate neighbourhood I went forward to reconnoitre the main-road which we were bound to cross in the next hundred yards or so. My costume lent itself better to this kind of work than did the garb of either of my companions, being as it was of a light brown colour whereas theirs was dark blue or black.

The road was all clear and we got across safely, and continued our march until we reached another road which we crossed safely also, but this time only just in time to avoid a woman on a bicycle.

Blank then went along the edge of the road to look at the sign-post near by, and we two lay fifty yards from the side of the road, bitten all over by the mosquitos which swarmed here.

He returned with his information, and off we went.

From this place we made our way so as to pass to the north of a village and strike the Weser bank immediately north of a small town, from which we hoped to steal a boat. We were now among cornfields and got held up until it became quite dark by the presence of various Germans in the fields. We had our evening meal while we waited and felt that the local Germans were very inconsiderate in being in their fields at this hour. However, it was a Saturday night, so it was not so surprising after all that they kept such late hours.

When all was quiet we continued our advance, cutting across corn-fields and getting nice and wet from the dew in so doing.

Striking a village, we walked through it and then took the wrong road for a mile or so before finding out our mistake. On getting on to our correct line again we crossed a level-crossing and began to pass through the outskirts of a small town. Turning north to avoid this we arrived at another level-crossing, where we halted to discuss our route. Suddenly the door of the cottage by the level-crossing opened and a man came out. He stood and stared at us, ten paces away.

We quietly moved off and got to the edge of a dense copse, where we doubled on our tracks as quickly as possible, crossing the railway some two hundred yards from the cottage. In crossing a railway one has to be particularly careful not to trip over the signal wires in the darkness. We made some noise on this occasion, as we did not know of the wire's existence and naturally crashed right into it. We did not wait to see if our noise had drawn anyone or not, but pushed ahead rapidly. A few hundred yards and we were on the bank of the river which flowed swiftly by, looking a pretty formidable obstacle in the light of the moon.

We had agreed to have a rapid search for a boat, and then, if we had no luck, to swim the river as soon as possible. Fortune favoured us, however, and we found a large ferry-boat moored to a post within one hundred yards of the place where we had first debouched on the river's bank. It did not take us long to get aboard and push off into the middle of the stream. Fox, an expert punter, took on the task of getting the boat across, although his bad hands suffered somewhat in the process. Enjoying our ride in the boat we let her drift down-stream for a mile or so. We felt extremely happy at this piece of good fortune and discussed quite seriously what we should have for dinner the first night in town, when we got back. The banks fairly flew past and it was not very long before we had left the farm, near to which we had discovered our boat, a long way behind us. Our free ride over, we chose a landing-place.

Fox brought the boat in towards the western side, and I agreed to go up the bank first in order to make sure that there were no Boche sentries patrolling the top of it. When the boat struck the bank where it was covered with bushes, I jumped out and forced my way up to the top, to find it all clear of Germans.

Now occurred what nearly proved to be a tragic episode, but it fortunately ended more comically than otherwise.

Coming down the slope again I put my foot on a rotten piece of bank which gave way, with the result that I went crashing into the bushes. Fox, thinking that the Germans had seized me, and that the noise he heard was made by my fighting with them, pushed the boat off into the river again, he and Blank lying flat on the bottom of it. When I got up I saw the boat swirling away down-stream, apparently empty and absolutely out of control.

For an awful moment I imagined that Blank had fallen overboard and had clutched Fox in doing so, and that now the two of them were drowning each other in the mud at the bottom of the river. I shouted, softly at first, and then louder and louder, but got no answer. The boat still drifted down-stream until it was lost to sight round a bend.

Here was a pretty state of affairs; all the water bottles were in the boat I knew, and my companions were Heaven knows where. Thinking it over, I decided that they might still be in the boat and that they had seen Germans or heard their voices. This decided me to remain still and quiet for an hour in the hopes of something turning up.

After half-an-hour or so, I saw two figures coming along the bank towards me and found on shouting to them, that it was indeed Fox and Blank. They had heard me shout before, but had thought it was meant for a warning to tell them to clear out. We were very relieved to have this episode over. They had brought all the water-bottles on with them and then turned the boat adrift, and watched it float down-stream. We could afford now to laugh at the whole thing, but for all that it was a far from pleasant experience.

However, the main thing which ran through our minds was the fact that the difficult crossing of the Weser was a thing of the past, and we could now reasonably hope to reach the frontier and have a chance to compete with its special difficulties, whereas prior to crossing the Weser it had been a presumption to do so.

CHAPTER VIII

THE RAILWAY TRACK

Sunday, 24th June. Leaving the Weser and travelling westwards for a mile or so we were exceedingly surprised to find that we had come close to the river again. For a moment we thought that perhaps we had got off our bearing, but our compass showed that we were right, and the stars checked the accuracy of the compass. In reality we had struck a great loop in the river and our westerly route led us close to it again.

Crossing cornfields and extensive areas planted with roots of all kinds, we got thoroughly soaked with dew well above our knees.

Fox and I both suffered considerably from our sore feet, and it seemed to me that my boots shrank a bit every time they got wet.

It had now begun to get fairly light and the coming day promised well to be fine. Being a Sunday we had naturally to think of what difference to our plans this might make. Germans we knew often go out into the wilder parts of the country when they have a day off, and in addition to scattering abroad the usual litter which always marks the presence of holiday-makers in all countries they wander into all sorts of out of the way places, and by so doing constitute a definite danger to be guarded against by the fugitive.

Realising this we were desirous of finding a particularly safe retreat for the hours of daylight.

Leaving the flat country immediately west of the river, we began crossing an undulating stretch of heath-land, which gave place after two or three miles to pastureland and corn.

Here it was that Blank, who had been in a prison camp situated in this district, declared that he knew of a railway running from somewhere close to our position at that moment.

We decided to try to find it before we hid for the day, in order to know its exact whereabouts when we moved off that night.

Sure enough we came to a large cutting, and were able to get on to the convenient road we found waiting for us at the bottom of it without any great difficulty.

It was high time now to think seriously of a hiding-place. This was not forthcoming. Instead we seem to have entered a district packed with farms. This railway track had evidently been made with the express object of tapping this rich farming district.

At about 4.45 we suddenly became aware of a man behind us, following along the railway track some four hundred yards off. This drove us up the southern side of the cutting we were traversing at the moment, and away across country in a rapid search for good cover. Nothing turned up to suit us for some time and we were beginning to feel fairly desperate, as the Germans usually begin to milk their cows somewhere about 5 o'clock.

At last, after travelling at top speed for nearly half an hour, we found a thick plantation situated between two farms. Into this we crawled not feeling at all satisfied with the cover. It proved to be really dense, which was a blessing, and despite the cold, two out the three of us were very soon asleep after a hot drink.

We took it in turns to watch here, each doing a two hour stretch of sentry-go, and then four hours off. These hours of waiting were fearfully long and tedious, one could not sleep for very many hours, and then it was a case of sitting still till darkness fell, when further desire to rest had been killed.

Towards the evening of this Sunday we were again badly scared, by hearing dogs barking and the reports of shot-guns quite close to us.

Evidently the farmers were trying the hedges and small plantations hereabouts for rabbits. What if the dogs were put into our copse?

We discussed several murderous schemes. Eventually we thought that the remaining half of the tinned beef, which was to serve as our evening meal, might be used with good effect as a means by which any inquisitive dog's attention might be held while a dastardly attack could be made on it from behind. Our lethal weapons consisted of a pocket-knife of Fox's and a table knife of mine. Fortunately the dogs never came into our copse, so murder was not necessary.

Intending to begin our night's march at 10.30 p.m. we cautiously worked our way to the edge of our cover and Fox went on to scout. He came back shortly afterwards to say that we must wait as several Germans were still strolling about the fields.

It was not till 11 p.m. that the last of them went into a cottage some four hundred yards away, leaving the ground clear to us. We soon got back to our railway cutting and continued to walk rapidly in a westerly direction.

We were now very much in need of water and were fortunate in hearing the trickle of a small stream which ran at the bottom of the embankment.

Much refreshed by our drink and with full water bottles we pushed on.

Nothing very exciting happened during the night's march, but again we were badly rushed for a hiding-place in the morning.

Monday, 25th June. Not a sign of anything at all suitable presented itself. We looked at a new station building, and wondered whether, could we but get into it, it would prove a safe place for our nineteen hours of waiting. However, it did not stand the test of our discussion, so we moved on. It was now a case of going at top speed, and leaving the railway. We tried copse after copse only to find them all too open. At last, after considerably exceeding our time limit, we found an excellent place in which to hide. A small densely planted copse of trees of the Christmas-tree variety, situated in lonely fields, seemed to offer as good a place as we could wish, but had the disadvantage of being near no water.

"EVERY DARK CORNER SEEMED
TO CONTAIN A DOG"

The day passed off uneventfully, and we left our hiding-place at 10 p.m. striking the railway track shortly afterwards.

After a couple of hours' hard walking we rested for a few minutes, and lit cigarettes from the few precious ones that remained to us. It certainly was rather a risky thing to do, but as we carefully shaded the match and this part of the track was very enclosed, we did not fear very much on that score. On proceeding a mile or so Fox suddenly discovered that he had left the box of cigarettes, with a dozen or so still in it, on the stone on which he had sat.

He decided to go back, so we remained where we were and rested. Both box and cigarettes had English words on them, which was the chief reason of his return to search. Cigarettes with English names, etc., would mean "Englishmen" to the meanest Boche intelligence, which would not take long to develop into "escaped prisoners," and might in turn spell "search and pursuit."

He returned after being away nearly an hour, without the cigarettes. They were nowhere to be found.

Tuesday, 26th June. Dawn. We left the railway-line at about 2.30 a.m., as it had turned towards the south-west and joined another line.

Striking across country we made good progress until we approached a road. Here we had suddenly to dive into the nearest cover, as a trap containing two men drove past.

The spot into which I dived was a patch of stinging nettles with a hidden strand of barbed wire running through the middle of it! Blank dived in the open but fortunately was not seen, although conspicuous enough in all conscience.

The trap gone, we crossed the road and began to think of a hiding-place. This we did not find easily. Village followed village, and we could not get clear of this district of farms and cottages. It had now become broad daylight and we began to feel the desperate early morning sensation again. All the dogs in the country prowled around the farm-yards we passed, or so it seemed to us. A barn in the process of being filled with hay presented its inviting doors to us. Fortunately, although much tempted, we steered clear of it and continued our hunt.

Eventually, at about 5.15 we found a small copse of fir trees situated in pasture land, and were not sorry to get into it. It was bitterly cold, but we slept quite well.

CHAPTER IX

CROSSING THE RIVER HUNTE AND THE TOWN OF "DOGS"

After the morning's rest in the copse, and the great increase in warmth due to the sun, which soon caused us to feel very thirsty, we thought that a move during the afternoon would not be too risky as the country was of a very wild deserted appearance hereabouts, and our need of water was a matter to be dealt with as soon as possible. Accordingly at 3 p.m. we moved out of our hiding-place and very soon found a pump by a cowshed in a field. We drank and filled up our water-bottles and then hid again in a wood close by.

We were much worried while drawing water by a large herd of cows. They must have been very thirsty, as they crowded round us and whenever we moved towards them would gallop off for a few yards and then return.

We were afraid lest this behaviour on their part had been seen and would cause comment or even worse among any farm people who might be within view of the shed.

While lying hidden in the wood the sound of axes being used near us came to our ears. This was not very disturbing though, and we managed to pass a peaceful evening talking in the sunlight; quite a restful feeling stole over one; life for the moment was not the strenuous thing it had been for so many days.

The songs of birds and the buzzing of insects combined to lend a peaceful atmosphere to the surroundings. A deer appeared from the interior of the wood and quietly went about its feeding as if we did not exist. If only one could have known that the future was to be favourable, and that success was to crown our effort, it would have been even extremely enjoyable in that wood.

But misgivings and forebodings of evil were natural to us, and robbed us of the full amount of pleasure we might otherwise have enjoyed in such a pleasant entourage.

In the evening clouds began to drift up and eventually a slight drizzle began to descend, but not sufficiently copious to make us miserable.

At 10 p.m. we began our night's march, and worked forward to the western edge of the wood; from here we were able to look out over a wide stretch of pasture and cornland.

In the distance a railway line crossed the field of vision. A beautiful wild sunset cast a golden light on the country-side. A road ran close by the wood and we waited till the light should die in the sky before crossing it.

At last we were well away, and reached the railway we had previously seen, which we crossed a moment before two trains rumbled past. One of these was a heavily laden munition train, the other much lighter. After leaving the railway we took to a lane which eventually brought us out into the main road. Just before debouching on to this, Fox and I both heard a bicycle coming along the road, and we dived into the long grass at the side of the road. Blank, however, did not hear it and blundered straight into the cyclist, a woman, before he could stop.

Fortunately his "Guten Abend" was sufficiently German to pass, and the cyclist continued her way after answering him with the same words. We caught him up some ten minutes later, and then cut across country. A farm loomed up in front of us and we bore to one side of it, but not before the ubiquitous dog made the night hideous with its barking, so we passed on with as little noise as possible.

Soon after this a stream barred our way. A rapid search for a bridge did not bring one to light, so there was nothing for it but to get wet. However, Fox had a plan whereby two of us might be saved a wetting. He being the heaviest was to strip and stand in the middle of the stream while we crossed over, using his shoulders as a stepping-stone. When he got into the stream he found the bottom very muddy and the water came up to his chest.

I was to try the 'stunt' first. All the food bags, etc., were carried across, and then Fox stood ready to do his part. Stepping well out from the bank and placing one foot on his shoulder I reached down until I could catch hold of his hands and waited for his signal. At the word, I sprang, he simultaneously throwing me, and before I had time to realise anything, I found myself rolling over and over on the other side. The timing had been perfect and I had landed completely dry.

Blank was also got across successfully, and then the two of us pulled Fox out. But not without an effort, as one of his feet had got well embedded in the mud. He told us then that a large stone had prevented the other from getting similarly stuck.

Rapid marching was the order after this episode, and we covered a great distance in an extraordinarily short space of time.

We had omitted to fill our water-bottles at the last stream, and this burst of speed soon made us painfully aware of it. Finally we found some appalling water in a ditch at the road side, but only by digging a hole in the mud, could sufficient be got to fill a water-bottle. This water was naturally very muddy and full of those little beetle things that rush about the surface of stagnant pools—'water-boatmen'—I think they are called. I know I felt them running about the inside of my mouth when I drank.

Wednesday, 27th June. We were now approaching the Hunte river. This river is not very large, but is sufficiently formidable to require swimming if no bridge or boat is used. Therefore, finding on a map that a bridge crossed it at a certain spot miles from anywhere of importance, or anywhere at all for that matter, we had decided that it would in all probability be unguarded.

It was clear now that we were getting near this bridge. A dense mist overhung the valley through which the river ran, and made it easier for us to approach. I, having the best coloured costume and the lightest footwear, went a few yards ahead of the others to reconnoitre the bridge.

Cautiously approaching it, I was delighted to find that no guards were posted there, and we got across without difficulty. A few miles further on, our westerly line would bring us to a small country town, which must be nameless.

The country in this district was covered with corn, and knowing that a detour through these corn-fields to avoid the town would mean an hour or more of delay, we decided to run the risk and walk through the streets of the town itself.

All went well at first. The town seemed absolutely deserted, and we crept along in the shadows where practicable, choosing the dusty gutters and grassy patches at the side of the road in order to make as little noise as possible. We reached a kind of square towards the centre of the town, when Blank stumbled over a cobble-stone, a not unusual thing for him to do, which called forth various cryptic whispers from Fox; at that moment, out of a dark shadow on the right of the road, a great dog slowly emerged.

With hackles bristling and teeth bared he approached us, emitting savage growls. The only thing to be done was to walk straight past him making no noise. This we did, passing within two yards of the beast. It seemed to scare him for he stopped and when we had got well past began barking furiously.

Then it was that we discovered that the place was stiff with dogs. The din made by their combined barking was absolutely awe-inspiring. Every dark corner seemed to contain a dog.

Shapes flitted about near us, and one got the impression that they were collecting for a combined attack. It was no use going quietly now, so we put on speed and rushed through the place. Nobody came out into the streets, however, but the blinds over a lighted window were pulled aside, disclosing a face which peered out into the darkness at us.

After ten minutes of apprehension we gained the outskirts of the town, where the last of our doggy foes stood to meet us right in the centre of the road.

He was a large bristly animal and had a particularly nasty note in his growl.

We adopted the same procedure with him, and after waiting till we were almost on top of him he turned tail and fled.

We were clear of that town now, but vowed never again to run such a risk.

My experience of German dogs at night, by no means slight, causes me to think that they bark so much and so often, generally at nothing, that their owners take absolutely no notice of them. It is a case of "Wolf! Wolf!" in real life.

Of course, the tired-out state of an over-worked and insufficiently fed population must make rising in the small hours of the night, to see what the dog is barking about, even less popular than is usually the case. Anyway we profited.

Leaving the vicinity of the town at the same great speed for fear of pursuit, we soon placed several miles between the scene of this, our latest fright, and the wooded country we now struck.

It had become light by now, so we had to search for a hiding-place at once. This we found in a hollow filled with undergrowth, an offshoot of a wood surrounded by corn and potato fields.

We were very tired, but quite pleased with our progress, as we must have done well over twenty miles from the time we began our march at 10 p.m. A day of sun and warmth made the drying of clothes, socks, and boots an easy matter.

CHAPTER X

EXIT BLANK, SHEDS

A quiet day amid peaceful surroundings counteracted the effects of the excitement of the previous night. We slept quite well by reason of the good conditions, and but for the soreness of Fox's heel and my left ankle would have felt extremely fit. We were guilty during the afternoon of a piece of carelessness which nearly gave us away. Fox and Blank were near the edge of our hiding-place, and went to sleep with some of our kit spread about the ground round them. I was asleep further inside our cover, but my boots were with theirs drying in the sun.

Suddenly Fox woke up and saw a woman not fifty yards from them, planting something in the field and gradually moving in our direction as she worked. Waking Blank and seizing all the kit he could find he crawled into the depths of our hiding-place, followed by Blank who had got hold of other portions of our impedimenta. An hour or so later the woman departed and we found that one of my boots had remained in the open all the time. We decided that in all probability she had not seen it, and so had no fears of discovery due to her.

The night's march began at 10 p.m., but it proved to be too early an hour for such night-birds as we. Hardly had we moved two hundred yards from our cover, when a youth with a shot-gun, prowling round in search of rabbits, saw us from about sixty-yards away. We legged it and soon left him wondering what three rough-looking men with heavy bags, and of military age, were doing in that part of the country.

Making excellent progress that night, we crossed a wild stretch of heath in the early hours of the morning, and then got back to more of the abominable corn-land again. Crossing a railway and passing a cottage by the level-crossing we were greeted with the usual barking of a house-dog.

Thursday, 28th June. It was now high time to think of our hiding-place for the day. Nothing presented itself and we carried on with our rush westwards. Cover after cover we examined without finding what we wanted, and at last, hearing German voices not far off, we were forced to adopt the first thing which presented itself.

This proved to be a wood cut up with broad drives, with hardly any undergrowth in it.

We had to make the best of a bad job, and by making a kind of zareba of dead branches, some sort of cover from view from anyone more than fifty yards away was possible.

The sound of voices on all sides of the wood, which was only about 200-300 yards wide, and the yapping of the ever-present dogs, together with the fact that half-cut hay-fields touched the wood on two sides, made it imperative that we should have a sentry all the time. After a hot drink and a breakfast of beef and biscuits, which made us feel a little warmer, Fox and I lay down to sleep. Blank, who had asked for the first watch, for the two hours till 7 a.m., because he said he was too cold to sleep, was to undertake the duties of sentry. It is necessary to state here that, now we were so rapidly approaching the Ems river, Blank had begun to have serious misgivings about his ability to swim it.

We had fully made up our minds that there was to be no looking for boats or building of rafts for that river. The Germans, we knew, were certain to have this obstacle well guarded, and the only chance of success, and that but a slight one, lay in dashing through the watchers and swimming it. Blank had spoken of trying to find a boat in order to tackle the Ems on his own.

Well, Fox and I went to sleep feeling fairly secure with a sentry to warn us in time to get away should we be discovered. After about an hour we both woke up, instinctively feeling something was wrong. Blank had disappeared. On looking out of our hiding-place I saw him lying fast asleep in the full sunlight, right in the middle of the drive some fifty yards away.

We woke him up by throwing some pieces of wood until we hit him.

He came back to our hiding-place, and naturally Fox and I felt much annoyed that the trust we had put in his watching should have been betrayed. This incident, combined with Blank's fears for the future, when in all probability he would have to swim the Ems, made it imperative for us to come to some arrangement. It was decided that Blank should go on by himself from this point. We arranged to divide up our supplies and equipment so that he should have a third.

    Accordingly, after I had copied the map for him, all was ready by noon for his departure. Taking a third of the food, a water-bottle, compass, and a copy of the map, he left us, determining to push on by day as he was unable to find his way at night by himself. The line he decided to follow involved his following the main-road through ———, a large military centre. However, he hoped to get through this place, trusting to his luck, civilian clothes and a fair knowledge of German to assist him.

    Leaving us lying in our hiding-place, he was soon out of sight, and we saw or heard nothing more of him.

    At about 10 o'clock we, Fox and I, began our march. We struck northwards now in order to get off the line taken by Blank in the morning, in case he had been caught and had thus made the Germans more wide-awake.

    Proceeding at a decent pace we soon came in sight of some sheds which lay directly on our line of march. Being curious and feeling much more confident, as we were now only two, we decided to go as close to the sheds as we dared in order to get a good look at them.

    We were able to see them excellently, although we never got very close to them. What prevented us from approaching any nearer was the sound of a concertina issuing from a hut a hundred yards from us. German voices could also be heard, so we considered that we had done all that could be done and left the place exceedingly rapidly, feeling that we should be safer when we had put a few miles between these sheds and ourselves. A very wooded country now lay before us, and we made good progress by walking along the fire cuts and drives, which conveniently ran east and west. We soon struck a main-road, which we followed for some time. While proceeding along this a cyclist dashed past us making practically no noise, so we had no time in which to take cover. He looked at us when passing, but it was so dark under the trees, that he could not have got any impression of our appearance.

By now both of us were suffering very much from our feet, and on leaving the main-road and taking to rough tracks over wild country we suffered intensely owing to the inequalities of the ground.

Friday, 29th June. At about 4.30 a.m., thoroughly tired out, but pleased with the distance travelled that night, we found a place in which to hide.

A rest till noon, and then feeling that we had barely sufficient food for the distance still to be covered, we decided to try and push forward a mile or so during the afternoon in the rough country of that distance. Leaving our hiding-place at about 3 p.m. we cautiously crossed a road and continued slowly working forward till about 6 o'clock. Here, finding excellent cover in a very thick fir plantation, we halted until dark.

We were well north now of our original route, and we must have been more than twelve miles away from the east and west line Blank had taken.

At first we had been worried over the idea of his probable capture affecting us also. But remembering that the Germans did not know that the parties had amalgamated, and were looking for one single man and two in a separate party, for the original report from the camp must have started the existence of two separate escapes, we felt much reassured. If they caught Blank they would naturally conclude that they had re-captured me, and that the original party of two might be anywhere, and nowhere in particular.

CHAPTER XI

TWO DAYS TO THE EMS

Leaving our secure hiding-place at 10 p.m. as usual, we made good progress until we came to a stream which had evidently been widened artificially, as it had the appearance of a canal at the point at which we struck it. It was quicker we thought to strip and cross at once than to hunt up and down, perhaps without avail, for a possible bridge.

I took to the water first. It was up to my shoulders and the bottom was muddy. I went across to try it without any of our possessions with me. It was lucky I did so, as at the other side of the stream I got into very bad mud and had a hard job to get out of it. By dint of half swimming, half clambering among the thick reeds on the edge of the river I managed to get over, but I had found out the best way to tackle it, and went back to the other side quite easily.

Taking the bulk of our possessions tied roughly together on the big bag with me, I got safely across and deposited them on the other side by my second trip.

Another journey, and all our gear was across. Fox being a heavy man could naturally do none of this work as the mud was too treacherous. As it was, in attempting to cross himself, he got badly stuck near the bed of reeds on the other side.

With my hand to help him and by making use of the reeds with arms and body, he struggled clear at last, by no means sorry to be on firm ground again.

Quickly dressing ourselves we got away in very little time, and made rapid progress.

Our map was very faulty in its description of this part of the country. Villages had sprung up lately perhaps, and as it was an old map they were not included in it.

The main result of this to us was that we discovered here at unexpected moments villages and collections of farms in front of us. We took them all as they came, driven to great speed by the threat of having to reduce our food rations. As usual our canine foes advertised our movements everywhere, but we had become thoroughly used to them by now, and took little or no notice of them.

The sign-posts at the road-junctions in this particularly old-world district were very ancient, often written in old German characters. To read them it was frequently necessary for me to mount on Fox's shoulders in order to get a closer look at blurred and faded words.

These villages, seen as they were by the light of a nearly full-moon, gave one the impression of being extremely beautiful. The houses were all old. Bulging walls, practically all containing supports and cross-pieces of old timber, and low eaves were common.

It was a very out-of-the-way track we had chosen, and one wondered whether we had unwittingly come across a collection of something quite out of the ordinary in the way of old-fashioned villages. I should like to have seen them by day. I expect some of these old places could produce a very fine collection of really old furniture if they were searched by a connoisseur.

While creeping through a village we got a bad fright in the early hours of the morning. Without warning we heard the ringing of a high-noted bell quite close to us.

The mystery of this was rather alarming until we solved it.

A few yards farther on we passed an old church in the side of the road; from the windows of this a faint light was shining. The bell rang again, and we located the sound as having come from the church. Evidently an all-night mass for the dead must have been in progress.

On clearing the village we seemed to leave civilisation behind us and entered an area of wild moorland. At first here and there quaint-looking houses were dotted about, but even these we left behind in our rush westwards over this moor.

Saturday, 30th June. By this time it was fairly light and we had covered a great distance in a very short space of time. A hiding-place was forthcoming when we decided to rest, and with a plentiful supply of water not very far away we managed at last to get a good hot drink before sleeping.

The wildness of the country and the need for speed moved us on again at about 3 p.m. Excellent water was abundant in all the low land in this undulating moorland district, and after a good drink we felt very strong in preparation for what we decided must be a great march before we rested again.

While following a rough track over the heather-covered slopes, a young hare foolishly sat down in a tuft of heather a short distance ahead of us. This we proceeded to stalk, and thinking of the possible food supply in front of us we went very carefully for it. I took a detour round it so as to occupy its attention, while Fox, armed with a water-bottle held by the strap, warily approached it direct. He got to within two yards of it before up it got.

A wild swipe with the water-bottle missed it by six inches. The hare galloped off, while our water-bottle let its valuable contents run out rapidly. However, Master Hare had not apparently had enough of it, for he again squatted in a tuft some two hundred yards farther on. The same plan of attack was carried out, and again Fox got to within striking distance.

This time, feeling that the strap had only retarded the attack, he hurled the whole thing at the hare, narrowly missing it, but this time scaring it so much that it disappeared in the distance at a great pace.

At about 10 p.m. we got near a village we had been making for, with the object of striking a road. This village, although nothing very important, proved to be the point of concentration of roads and tracks crossing the moor. In making a careful detour round the northern outskirts of it we suddenly came upon three men in dark clothes, standing on one of these tracks. Turning sharply to the north we made for a wood a mile or so away, and watching them carefully out of the corners of our eyes we slunk along rapidly. They did not really follow us, although they took a few paces in our direction.

Having gained the wood we made a circle through it and were able to come back to the vicinity of the village well away from the three men. We could still see them, but then we knew where to look and they would have had to be visual marvels to see us, peeping as we were over the top of the corn, which was plentiful all round this village. At last we got on to our right road, which led us to the end of the moorland and eventually landed us in a swampy bottom cut up with dykes and small streams. Here we floundered about in a hopeless manner in the darkness. Feeling thoroughly tired and cold owing to the rain which had begun to descend an hour or so previously, we got into a cowshed and decided to have as many hot drinks, etc., as we could manage, and push ahead as soon as we could see sufficiently well to do so without wasting time. I think we had about three brews each. It was marvellous the effect this had on us. We both felt absolutely fresh again, and quite strong enough for another long stretch before sleeping.

Sunday, 1st July. When sufficiently light we set off, passing a village in the daylight, the track leading out of this difficult country being easily found now, though it had eluded all our efforts during the hours of darkness.

A large hill lay before us, and we decided to go to the top of it so as to get from there a view of the country which lay before us. It was a stiff climb and we reaped our reward. A magnificent view greeted us. It was indeed a sight of the promised land, as we remarked at the time.

This hill was the last piece of high ground, or for the matter of that of any ground not dead flat, on the way to the frontier.

We could see the valley of the Ems and the funnels of a steamer which we knew must be on the river itself.

The flat country had an almost sea-like appearance, spreading as it did to a regular horizon, where the country became a misty grey line.

A twenty minutes' rest here, and on we went.

We were feeling our feet badly again now, and decided to rest on the lower slopes of the hills. On the way down we put up a fox. We had been extremely surprised all along at the scarcity of game in the wild country we had traversed.

"FOX LED THEM OVER THE WORST PIECES OF BOGGY GROUND HE COULD FIND"

Beyond a few deer, our hare, a black-cock, and a few duck which we heard in a corn-field, absolutely nothing else showed itself or gave any sign of its existence. As we had gone quietly for the greater part of the distance, it was astonishing that we should have surprised no rabbits out feeding in the early mornings.

We came to the conclusion that, from an English standpoint, there is little or no game in these parts of Germany.

At 5 a.m., finding a good thick copse of small fir-trees, we lay up for a rest. We were now about six miles from the river Ems, which again was some ten miles from the frontier. We decided that the Ems and the frontier itself should be crossed on the same night.

Therefore, in order to allow enough time for such a large programme, we must cross the Ems at the beginning of the night; this meant that the six miles which lay before us now before arriving at the river, had to be done before dark. We proposed to move forward at 5 p.m. A good rest and a large meal worked wonders on our tired bodies, and we felt fit for our last great effort by the hour selected.

Before moving off, however, we decided to make a "cache" of all our superfluous luggage, taking with us only food for twenty-four hours, with a bottle of milk each as an emergency ration, and the water-bottles. The remainder, which was not much now, we hid carefully in case we failed and had to come back for reserve food.

The bag we also left, as that stamps the escaped prisoner more than anything else. We each now had a bundle done up with a coloured handkerchief.

The wild country still stretched westwards until it gave place to a wet valley cut up into rough hay-fields and meadows of rank grass. While walking quietly along a rough grass road here, we suddenly saw a cart with two men in it come out of a field behind a hay-stack some four hundred yards from us. Deciding that to avoid them, when they must have already seen us, would be a very suspicious act, we walked straight ahead. When level with them the old man driving shouted out something to us; we stopped and he repeated his sentence. For the life of me I couldn't make out a single word he said. He had a squeaky voice and spoke a vile patois, but it sounded like no language I had ever heard.

His third attempt to make us understand something had no more success, but Fox, who hardly knew a word of German, walked two paces towards him and shouted "Yah"! "Yah"! With that we walked off, leaving the old man and his youthful companion gaping at us.

We discussed the matter as we walked away, and both came to the conclusion that he had used the word "Landsturm." From this we made up a nice theory. We imagined that the old man had thought that we had been called up for Landsturm service, and were trudging off to the nearest town with our bundles in our hands to join up. They still stood and looked at us, and we had our beautiful theory badly smashed a minute or two later. We suddenly came to the end of the cart-track and found a ditch full of water bordered with a barbed wire fence in front of us. As they were still looking at us, we followed the ditch down for a short distance and then crossed it without hesitation, hoping to give the impression that we knew what we were about.

They drove on then, and we turned our thoughts to other matters. Some distance further on we came across a youth of about sixteen who was in charge of a flock of sheep. When we were quite close to him his dog must have done something to upset the youth's Hunnish temper, as the beast got a fearful hiding.

Blow after blow, accompanied with torrents of Hun oaths, were rained on the wretched animal's back by this child of Kultur, who was armed with a heavy stick. To interfere would have been madness on our part, so we passed on. For the next mile we could hear the poor beast's howls.

A swampy mile or so had now to be covered, and then we got on to the edge of a fir wood, which ran down to a road and railway. These we reached and crossed safely, finding ourselves once again in farmland and a country of hedges and dykes. When we judged that we had still a mile or so to do before striking the river we halted and had our last meal, hidden under a good thick bush which constituted part of a hedge at the side of a rough track.

Setting out at 10 p.m., before it was really dusk, we followed a grass track westwards and very nearly got ourselves caught by a piece of carelessness.

CHAPTER XII

THE CROSSING OF THE RIVER

The river winds about considerably. It was into a canal that we suddenly walked on turning a corner of a rough track. A bridge lay right before us, with a sentry on it, who must have seen us at the same moment as we saw him. Turning back we retraced our steps, but not before we had seen two German patrols walking along the canal bank. Leaving our track we got back to our previous hiding-place, intending to wait until it was quite dark before attempting to cross the river some distance to the north. Hardly had we got into our bush when a cyclist soldier passed along the track along which we had been walking a minute or two before. This alarmed us somewhat, but we deemed it best to remain hidden till it should be darker.

While waiting we found and finished off our tin of milk, and discussed plans in a whisper. We allowed half an hour or so to elapse and then started off again; this time following a track running parallel to the river, northwards. We had done a mile or so, when, just before crossing another grass-road which led to the east, I saw the spiked helmet and rifle of a German soldier silhouetted against the sky, and moving rapidly from west to east. This turned us back, and we hoped then to be able to get eastwards across country until we could make a detour further northwards and regain the river bank.

Entering a field we got half-way across it when two horses, taking fright at something, galloped away from the far corner straight towards us. We now lay down and discussed matters. Germans were north of us, east of us, and south of us, we knew, and the river to the west of course would be guarded.

A quarter of an hour later, a weird cry, something like that of a curlew or peewit, but not exactly either, came to our ears from the north-west near the river. It was repeated from immediately north of us, and then north-east. From there the cry seemed to come from the east, moving southwards, until at a point south-east of us it was repeated time after time for two or three minutes, until taken up again further to the south, eventually ending again at the river, to our south-west.

I had heard rumours and talk about a system the Germans are supposed to have for guarding their frontiers from fugitives, while I was in prison. This system had been called a "fan" or "cordon." It now occurred to me that these bird-like cries had been all round us in a ring. It did not take much thinking to connect the Germans we had seen, the imitation cries, and our known presence in this district. The more we thought the more certain we felt that these Germans we had seen hurrying eastwards had been sent out expressly to form a fan-like formation, in which they hoped to hold us against the river till daylight should allow them to search the ground for us. The bird-like calls would be just the thing to indicate to the commander of this formation the exact whereabouts of his men and the continuity of the cordon, without being a suspicious fact to any hapless wretch caught inside, who did not happen to know the real notes of the birds imitated.

What was to be done? Should we try and break through the cordon, northwards or eastwards, by striking across country? This plan did not commend itself to us, as we should have had to get through thick hedges and wade through dykes innumerable without making any noise at all, an impossibility on a still moon-lit night such as it was. We decided to wait till 1.30 a.m., to give them time to get sleepy. An hour's sleep in a ditch, and then do something, was our plan.

Monday, 2nd July. Moving westwards a little, we came to a farm close by, and got the idea of hiding somewhere in a hay-loft and waiting till the next night, when perhaps no cordon would be round us, before attempting to cross the river. The farm was quite deserted, except for the cattle and horses, etc., which we could hear in the buildings. We tried now to open the doors of the barns and sheds, without avail. They had no locks, but open them we could not. We tried everywhere for a long time without the slightest success. At last our combined efforts forced a door open, and we got a nasty fright. A great pig galloped out past us and went off grunting into the darkness of the field. The inside of this building was no good, as it was a piggery and only held bare stalls, nearly all of which were already populated.

A cart of the kind used to convey pigs to market next attracted Fox, and he got into it to try it as a hiding place.

It was by no means a good place, as, although the cart was an ancient one and the farm people would probably not require it, the possible arrival of dogs with the men who would undoubtedly turn up in the morning to see to the animals in the farm, would lead to a nerve-racking experience, if not to actual capture.

While Fox reposed at the bottom of the cart I searched round for water, so as to fill the bottles against our possible stay of eighteen hours in the cart. There were two pumps in the yard, but both were broken.

I could find no water anywhere. The whole farm was a mystery which we never solved.

Returning to the pig-cart I was told by Fox that it would never do, as he had already got cramp after only ten minutes in it. He got out and we noticed then that it was threatening to become light.

Deciding to risk all we left the farm, making for the river in the hopes of avoiding the Germans. Our marvellous luck again came to the rescue. From the farm ran a narrow path which we had not noticed before. This we took, and after going only a short distance along it suddenly struck the bank of the river proper long before we expected to do anything of the kind.

This path was so small and unimportant that it must have been overlooked and considered too unimportant to require guarding, as we saw no Germans thereabouts.

It did not take us long, now that we were on the bank of the river, to get on to a point of land jutting out into it, and taking cover in the long grass and bushes there.

The Ems flowed sluggishly at this point, and appeared to be about a hundred yards across.

We had made up our minds to leave all the not absolutely essential articles of clothing, etc., behind us here, and tie the things we must take with us to the tops of our heads and then swim.

Knowing that anyone found moving about the frontier line is a suspicious character to German frontier guards, and therefore asked to show his papers, although he might be in civilian clothes, I left my long coat of cotton stuff behind, preferring to rely on my old khaki coat which I wore underneath to make me less visible.

Fox had made the suggestion of the tying our clothes to our heads scheme, and I thought he knew all about it, so had not asked anything more about it. Now, taking our boots and coats off, we tied them into bundles, and Fox got his safely on to the top of his head and took to the water at once.

He looked a weird sight, swimming slowly on his chest.

I tied my boots to my waist-belt and then tried to balance my coat on to the top of my head. This would not work. Time after time it rolled off on to the grass. I suppose the top of his head is flatter than mine, but on mine the bundle would not stay. At last, desperate at seeing him on the other side of the river trying to land, I tied my coat on to my left shoulder with a large handkerchief to hold it there, knotted round my neck. Then I also took to the water, swimming on my right side, so as to keep my coat and its contents as dry as possible.

I had noticed that Fox was still stuck at his point of striking the other bank, and was evidently hung up by the dense bushes which hung well over the river at that point. This made me strike a little up-stream so as to make for a clearer place on the other bank.

This I reached and got ashore without difficulty.

Fox had found it extremely hard to get out of the river at all; in fact he had got to the other side to find that he could not get his feet on to solid ground, and had tried to pull himself ashore by clutching at the over-hanging branches with his hands. It was now that the bundle on the top of his head, well-behaved till that moment, came adrift and fell into the water, and getting under a submerged branch, while the big handkerchief which held it still remained round his neck, practically pulled him under. In this predicament he could not yell for me at the other side of the stream to come to his assistance for fear of giving our position away to the German river patrols. After a hard struggle he managed to pull himself into the bank and was able to get ashore.

This episode cost him his boots, as they became unhitched in his struggles with the bundle, and sank.

On his telling me this I was able to help him in his problem of footwear. Although leaving all unnecessary kit behind, I had by error put a spare pair of thick woollen socks into the pocket of my khaki coat and was now able to produce them.

He put them on over his own and we proceeded on our way towards the frontier, running and walking, both for the sake of warmth and also to make the best use of the hour or so of half-light that remained to us.

"THE GERMAN RELIEF PASSED WITHIN 200 YARDS OF MY HIDING PLACE"

CHAPTER XIII

ACROSS THE FRONTIER

During our rapid march we passed a few houses, and shortly afterwards began to cross an open moor which spread flat and wide in front of us. Our map showed a canal bordering the frontier itself, and it was along this canal that we anticipated having to avoid the line of actual frontier watchers.

We were desperately anxious to make the frontier line within the next half-hour, in order to avoid having to lie waiting for the next night within a mile or so of it, as so many unfortunate escaped prisoners have been caught while hiding near the frontier itself. This anxiety on our part was now the cause of our making an appalling error, which nearly ended disastrously for us both. When within a mile of a line of trees, which we decided must be along the canal bank and must practically define the frontier line, we suddenly saw two German soldiers advancing some thousand yards in front of us. Had they seen us? We dived to the ground and lay still, in the hope that we had not been seen. Soon there was no doubt whatever that we had been observed, as the two Boches came straight towards us at a steady walk.

We decided that by separating one or both of us might succeed in getting away from them, and so I crawled towards the north while Fox went off southwards towards a peat observation hut.

Fox was dressed in his dark blue suit still, and I had now got my khaki coat as my outside garment. The value of the khaki coat now came out.

They evidently saw Fox crawling and not me, as they very soon changed their direction slightly in order to go after him. Fox and I had crawled two hundred yards apart when he must have had no doubt that they were definitely after him, and I suddenly saw him get up and run off, away from the frontier direction.

He seemed to me to be keeping the hut between him and his German pursuers. The latter, probably oldish men, or wounded and not absolutely recovered, had no idea of running after him, and I suppose they knew that their shooting was not good enough to score a hit at a running-man four hundred yards from them. However, they followed his course at a brisk walk, passing me at some hundred to two hundred yards distance.

I saw them go to the hut, look in, and not finding anything in it of interest to them, continue their pursuit. Fox led them over the worst pieces of boggy ground he could find. Having no boots and very light footwear, by reason of the two pairs of socks being his all, he was able to do excellent "time" over the peaty soil.

The Germans got others to help them, and eventually had quite a number of Boches after him. Finding a hole in the ground which satisfied his requirements, Fox got into it and covered himself over with peat and heather.

The "field" now included dogs and cyclists. When the dogs had got sufficiently near him to cause real alarm a marvellous stroke of luck came to his assistance. A flock of sheep, grazing on the moor, wandered right across his track, drowning all scent and completely defeating all the efforts of the dogs to follow his line.

After lying shivering in his hole all day he commenced his final dash for the frontier at about 11 p.m., and crossed a mile or so to the north of the place at which I passed through the German frontier line, without seeing any sentries.

After the Germans had gone well past me in their hunt after Fox, I began to crawl again; but I made slow progress, as going on all-fours was out of the question, the vegetation being seldom more than eighteen inches high and in places considerably less. It was a most tiring game this sort of land-swimming, and I continued as long as I could each time I did a crawl, and then rested a space. In three hours I covered five hundred yards and then considered that I was far enough from the scene of our discovery to be safe, should the Germans return to see if anything of interest had been left at the place where they had first remarked Fox crawling.

I then lay still and began to feel fearfully cold on account of the soaking wet clothes clinging to me. I had a meagre meal. I had no water, so soon began to feel thirsty as the day began to warm up.

Sleep was out of the question, firstly on account of the cold and afterwards on account of the great heat when the sun got high.

I lay and thought of many things, mostly of that line of trees I could see ahead of me which I knew must be practically along the frontier line. The fear of recapture now became haunting. Up till then I had been fully prepared to find myself rounded up and then taken back to five months' solitary confinement, and I had managed to think of that probability with complete calm, as so few of the many who try to escape have the luck to get right through with it.

But now it was different, to be so near and know that twelve or fourteen hours of inactivity lay in front of one before the last great effort could be attempted, in which time one was powerless to move in the midst of this "Frontier" zone, was a nerve-shattering experience.

It would have been much better with a companion, as a whispered exchange of thoughts makes all the difference.

I wondered whether Fox had been caught and whether either of us would get over, but never dreamt that we should both have the marvellous luck to do so. While lying there waiting for night good luck again came to my assistance. The German relief for their posts actually on the frontier, marched across this open moor every two hours, and they passed along a track within 200 yards of my hiding-place, so that I could time their passing and was able to make plans accordingly.

They passed me regularly at half-past-five, half-past seven, half-past-nine, etc., and those that were relieved and had to return across the moor generally came by about three-quarters of an hour afterwards.

I was also able to watch them until they disappeared every time in a clump of bushes under the trees I had already noticed and conjectured must be along the frontier. Thus, I could fairly well assume that the position of one post was fixed. The afternoon wore on and I managed to pass some of the time by drying the compass, which had got full of water during the previous night's swim. With the exception of the regular passings of the Boche sentry-relief, the only other human being who showed himself was a shepherd, some five hundred yards away. I had an anxious time for a spell as he drove his sheep towards me, and I feared that if they came past me the dog might give me away. Fortunately he turned the flock homewards when still some three hundred yards from me. Evening slowly came, and the long hours of twilight gradually gave way to partial darkness. I cannot call it a stronger darkness than that, as the moon rose at once and the north never lost its weird light all night. I felt the want of sleep badly, but had not been able to sleep for even a quarter of an hour all day and now could not run the risk of waking too late, so had to do without it.

At 10.30 I came to the conclusion that I could move at last, and very pleased I was to stand up and rub my legs after my enforced uncomfortable position all day.

Setting out cautiously towards the frontier post that I had been able to more or less mark down, it was not very long before the mile or so of open that had to be covered was completed.

I thought that, were I to pass close to the post of which I knew the position, I must necessarily be as far from the unknown one on my right as possible.

At about 200 yards distance from what I judged to be the line of posts, I got on all fours and worked forward noiselessly. My khaki coat again stood me in good stead, as I must have been an extremely difficult object to see, even in the light which was at that time quite strong.

Once more my luck held good. When about midway between the posts, the Boche sentry on duty on my right, about whom I knew nothing, very obligingly chose that moment to stand up against the sky-line and begin singing "Die Wacht am Rhein." It was a fine night, which perhaps caused him to be jovial, but probably it was the result of smuggled spirits.

After singing a bit, my friend the sentry began shouting to his companion next beyond him.

This made matters easier for me, and I was able to crawl forward in full confidence. A dyke, at the bottom of which was a little water, had to be crossed, and then some rough fields.

Shortly after this I heard a patrol which I easily avoided in the corn. Several more dykes, the deepest water in any of them only reaching to my knees, had to be crossed, and I was once more on arable land. I must now have been two miles inside Holland, but now again I heard a patrol. This time a cyclist dashed along the road on hearing me, I suppose, and once again the same curlew noises began to spread themselves around me.

However, this time I knew about them and pushed on extremely rapidly, cutting across country and keeping to the cornfields where I knew I should never be followed and be very difficult to catch.

I soon left this danger behind, and then struck a pavé road and a railway line. The sleepers were wooden, whereas in Germany they are iron.

I felt now that I was across, but continued steadily on my way. Seeing a great number of powerful lights in front of me I made for them, and eventually reached them, to find that they belonged to a factory working at top pressure. Around this factory straggled a large village.

Tuesday, 3rd July. Here I found no guards and sat down to wait for daylight to show me the language of that village as indicated on the advertisements in the shop-windows. I had got in here at 3.30 a.m. and at 4.30 knew that the words in the shop-windows were Dutch and not Boche. What a great feeling of relief and rest it was!

The first man I saw was a soldier on a bicycle, to whom I made myself known. He was very quick to find me breakfast at the cottage of a fellow soldier of his. The latter refused all payment, and was an excellent fellow. Later I reported myself to the local policeman, and while talking to him heard Fox's voice. He had arrived two hours after me, after crossing the frontier a mile to the north of where I had passed the line. We were delighted to see each other, but at the time were not so tremendously struck by the fact that we had come together again. Of course it was an extraordinary thing to happen really, but we only realised that later.

At the moment we only thought of the fact that we were both safely across and would be home in due course, and that we had had the most marvellous luck that could well have come our way.

Fox had covered this distance, roughly a hundred and seventy miles as we did it, in twelve and a half days, and I had taken thirteen days and a few hours.

CHAPTER XIV

CONCLUSION

Breakfast was given us by the Dutch police official who had been our welcomer. They were very kind to us at his house, and we managed to get a small wash and we attempted to make ourselves look a little more respectable before going on to Rotterdam.

It was the first time I had seen a mirror for fourteen days, and when I saw what it told me I got a fright. A filthy, scrubby object met my gaze, and I was not sorry to get a shave that afternoon at the town before proceeding, and we stayed for the night and got baths.

We met nothing but kindness here.

Arriving at Rotterdam at noon next day, we said goodbye to our Dutch policeman and came under the excellent care of the British Consul there.

We landed in England after an uneventful voyage.

There are a few remarks to be made in conclusion.

Our phenomenal luck was the prime factor in making our attempt successful. Without that all-important item, attempt after attempt may be made without anywhere nearly approaching a success.

Our officer-prisoners, as a whole, by continuing their numerous and in many cases desperate attempts to escape, are doing a service to the country, and although nominally counted out of all useful work are doing valuable work, by causing the Germans to employ more guards to watch them than might otherwise be the case.

Prisoners are bound to be taken from all armies, and the unfortunates who have to undergo years of captivity should have the sympathy of all thinking persons. I myself feel great sympathy with those Germans who did two hundred miles in an open boat in their attempt to regain their country, and whom we brought back to more durance vile.

It is hardly sporting on the part of those people who declare that we should deal harshly with Germans who break away from their camp in this country. Fortunately, by agreement with the German Government, all heavy punishments for attempted escapes have been removed, so "the" one great pastime of prisoners of war will not cost so dear in future.

www.ingramcontent.com/pod-product-compliance
Lightning Source LLC
Chambersburg PA
CBHW072158100426
42738CB00011BA/2465